To Dear Kyla
with love from
Carol

SUNBIRD
PUBLISHING

First published 2004
2 4 6 8 10 9 7 5 3 1
Sunbird Publishing (Pty) Ltd (in association with the University of Pretoria)
34 Sunset Avenue, Llandudno, Cape Town, South Africa
Registration number: 4850177827

Copyright © 2004 published edition: Sunbird Publishing (Pty) Ltd
Copyright © 2004 text: University of Pretoria
Copyright © 2004 photographs: Mapungubwe Museum, University of Pretoria, with the exception of the following: Roger de la Harpe: p 6 (left); Hörst Klemm: pp 1, 13 (top left), 20 (top), 33, 63, 64 (top right), 66 (bottom right), 80; Andrie Meyer: p 5; Malita Moloney: back cover, pp 7 (bottom right), 10 (bottom right), 21 (top left and bottom right), 22 (bottom left), 37, 46 (top left), 48 (all), 49, 50 (top left), 59 (top right and bottom right), 60 (top right); E Raab: p 4; Andrew Salomon: front cover (all), pp 11 (right), 20 (bottom), 22 (top right), 23 (top left), 26, 45, 46 (bottom left and right), 47, 50 (right), 51, 52 (all), 53, 58 (left), 59 (top left and bottom left), 60 (left), 61, 69, 72 (all), 73, 80.

Publisher Dick Wilkins
Editor Reinette van Rooyen and Sean Fraser
Designer Mandy McKay
Production Manager Andrew de Kock

Reproduction by Unifoto (Pty) Ltd, Cape Town
Printed and bound by Tien Wah Press (Pte) Ltd, Singapore

All rights reserved. No part of this publication may be reproduced, stored in a retrieval system or transmitted, in any form or by any means, electronic, mechanical, photocopying, recording or otherwise, without the prior written permission of the copyright owner(s).

ISBN 1-919-93805-2

ACKNOWLEDGEMENTS
My thanks to the University of Pretoria, for its support and for its financial contribution to this book. Special thanks to Hörst Klemm for prereleasing his Mapungubwe photographs from his World Heritage Sites in Africa project. Thanks, too, to Nikki Haw, Dr André Breedt and, lastly, to my family and fiancée Johan Nel for his dedicated love over the years.

DEDICATION
To my grandfather, Edward Kirby

PREVIOUS PAGE *Gold beads on shallow ceramic bowl from Mapungubwe Hill.*

LEFT *Scattered through the Mapungubwe landscape are baobabs* Adansonia digitata.

ABOVE *Gold sceptre*

OPPOSITE *Manopi Hill, to the south of Mapungubwe Hill.*

OVERLEAF LEFT *Sketch of the Mapungubwe Valley.*

OVERLEAF RIGHT *An aerial view of Mapungubwe Hill from the southwest circa 1972, looking towards the base of the hill, known as the Southern Terrace.*

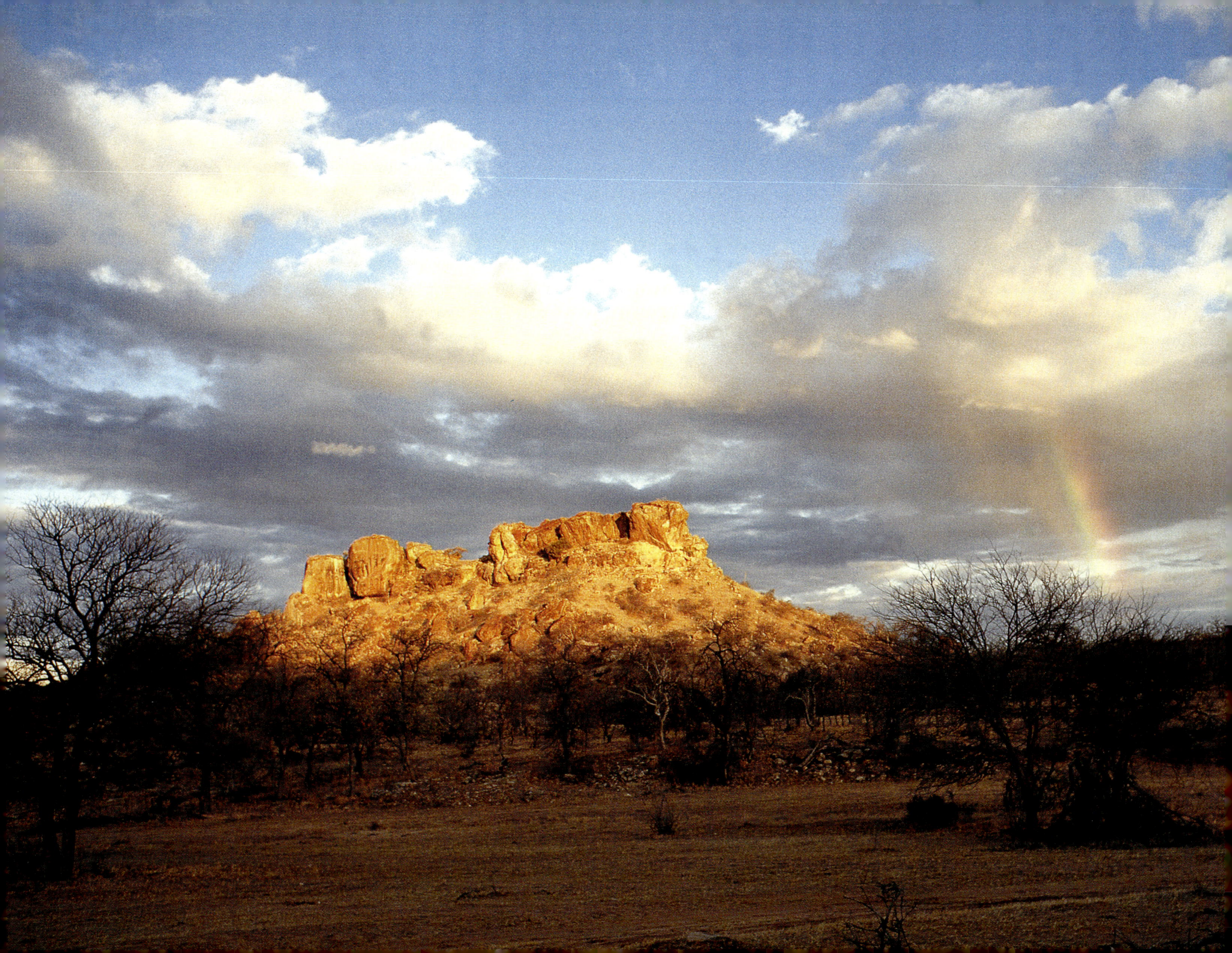

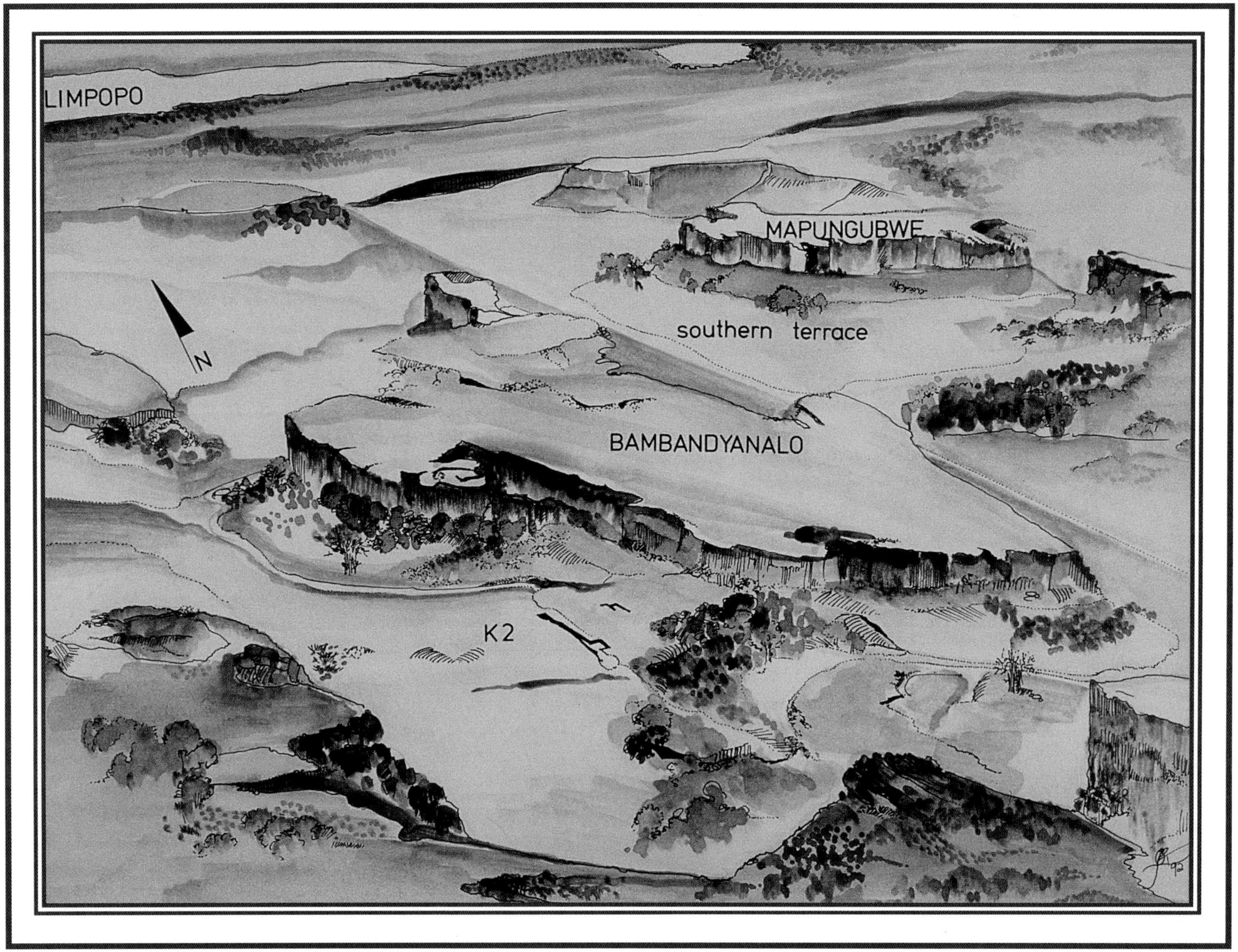
LIMPOPO
MAPUNGUBWE
N
southern terrace
BAMBANDYANALO
K2

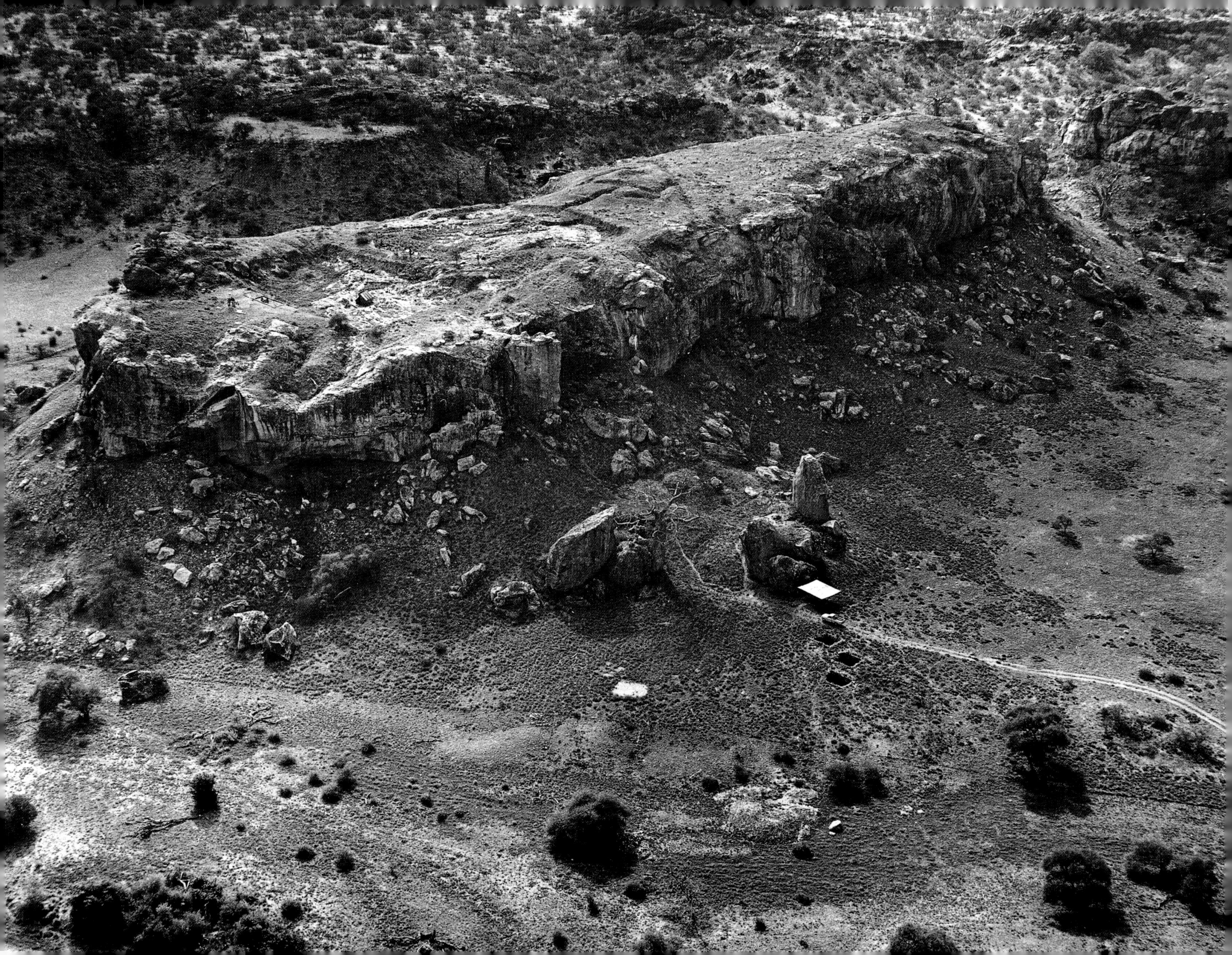

Introduction

Mapungubwe Hill rises 30 metres above the southern bank of the Limpopo River in the northernmost region of South Africa, in the Limpopo Province. For more than a thousand years, the 300-metre long hill served as a natural fortress and impregnable stronghold that entombed gold treasures of a forgotten kingdom.

The two main rivers of this region, the Shashe and Limpopo, converge a kilometre from Mapungubwe Hill to form the common international boundary between South Africa, Botswana and Zimbabwe.

Towards the end of the 19th century, European colonial powers moved into what was then Rhodesia to lay the cornerstone of what would one day be the Republic of Zimbabwe. For 10 centuries before that, the Bantu-speaking peoples migrated from central to southern Africa, where geography channelled them into a natural funnel. Here Mapungubwe was settled across a strategic communications trade route, where these two rivers and a natural north-south migration highway met.

Perhaps one of the most characteristic landscape features of Mapungubwe is the mopane bushveld. The mopane tree's leaves are easily identifiable by their butterfly shape and are a natural attraction for the edible mopane worm or *mashonza*, as it is known in TshiVenda. The Limpopo Valley is also famous for the bulky baobab tree, *Adansonia digitata*, which is casually scattered across the Mapungubwe landscape. Eerie-looking rows of baobabs are dotted against the skyline that is the view from Mapungubwe Hill looking south. To the north of Mapungubwe Hill, an elongated, natural black dolorite edifice stands out starkly, resembling a man-made wall.

ABOVE The Shashe and Limpopo rivers are the region's most significant, delineating the borders between South Africa, Zimbabwe and Botswana, and coming together about a kilometre from the Mapungubwe site.

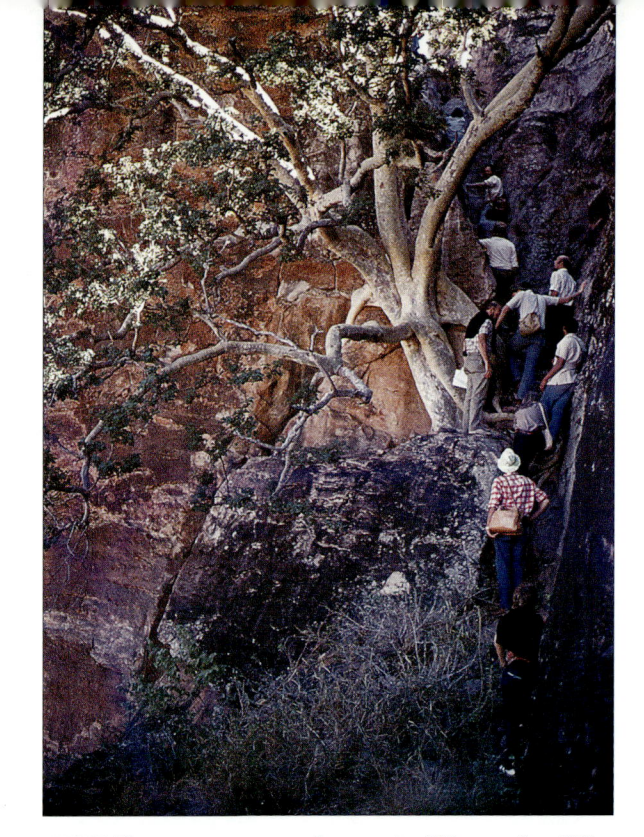

ABOVE The western ascent to the summit of Mapungubwe Hill passes an old fig tree, Ficus tellensis, *once known as* F. smutsii.

Mapungubwe Hill

Access to the top of Mapungubwe Hill is through a narrow passageway in the rock, which was formed at some forgotten time in the past by a block of rock shattering near the summit and 'calving', or slipping sideways to open up a cleft, so narrow and steep that only one person at a time can negotiate the route.

Surrounded by 30-metre cliffs on either side, it appears impossible to climb, offering no clues to the treasures and breathtaking views at the top. The entrance at ground level has been concealed for centuries by a huge *Ficus tellensis* (once known as *F. smutsii*, this wild fig tree was originally named after General Jan Smuts). Today an inconspicuous wooden stairway makes the journey to the summit easier.

ABOVE *Although Little Mapungubwe, also known as Little Muck, is a rather small sandstone hill, it dominates the view from Mapungubwe Hill, facing towards the south.*

The meaning of Mapungubwe

The meaning of the name 'Mapungubwe' remains a mystery. For decades, people have believed it to mean 'Place of the Jackal', a derivative of the Nguni word *mhungubwe*, or the TshiVenda word *punguvhe*, both meaning jackal. According to the BaLemba, the legendary Semitic race of southern Africa, Mapungubwe means 'the place where the molten rock flowed like a liquid or water', that is, the stones flowed like a liquid. Others assume that the meaning of Mapungubwe is analogous with that of Zimbabwe, whereby the -*bwe* means 'venerated stones or houses'. The name

ceramic cup

'Mapungubwe' will, however, remain open to interpretation and, as such, a mystery. Not being of Shona, Karanga or Venda origin, it instead suggests a dialect as yet unrecorded by linguists.

It is known that what is today the Limpopo Province was once a veritable melting pot of Bantu-speaking peoples, but there seems to be no clarity on this matter, which only serves to add to the obscurity surrounding Mapungubwe.

It is also ironic that Mapungubwe's name originates from the ramblings from an old, partially blind black man named Mowena, who, although he did contribute to the discovery of the site, did not actually lead the first discoverers to the Hill. Nevertheless, the name has stuck ever since.

The curse of Mapungubwe

It was the supernatural that elevated Mapungubwe to legend, a curse so ancient and deep-rooted that local inhabitants always regarded Mapungubwe Hill as taboo. To merely look or point towards it meant certain death. Consequently, the large region around the hill had been left uninhabited for centuries, as the Mapungubweans left it in the 13th century. Even at places far away from the hill, if the dreaded name 'Mapungubwe', was mentioned, people would turn their backs to it.

Locals believed that the hill was sacred to the great ancestral spirits whose treasures lay hidden for thousands of years. It was this tradition that led the discoverers to Mapungubwe.

The remoteness of the hill, surrounded by rocky ridges and home to giant baobabs, had been its best protection during these 700 years; but this same remoteness also facilitated the pillage of its treasures.

ABOVE *Gold beads were recovered from the royal cemetery found on Mapungubwe Hill.*

ABOVE *The Old Arts Building (1908), a national monument at the University of Pretoria, houses the Mapungubwe Museum.*

glass beads between brittle bone, it became clear that they had uncovered an ancient grave.

The 20-year-old Van Graan picked up the first piece of gold plate. Within minutes, the men had uncovered more, filling their hats to the brims with minute gold nails, gold beads and more. In his palm, Jerry held an intact squat gold rhino with a missing tail.

Some 50 years later, Jerry would see his miniature rhino on exhibition at the Gold Mine Museum in Johannesburg, only this time the torso would be missing its head as well as its tail.

The men removed several gold bangles from a skeleton. Unfortunately, many of the bones merely crumbled to dust on being exposed to the air. They found that the body's neck, arms and legs had also been surrounded by a large quantity of gold wire bangles. Under the skeleton's left arm was a black bowl, exquisitely made and polished, filled with gold and glass beads.

ceramic vessel

Where the skull had lain, pieces of curiously shaped gold plate were found, the convolutions of which suggested that they had adorned a wooden headrest for the skeleton.

It was there that the remains of another miniature gold rhinoceros were found, along with the torso and legs of other crafted animals.

Great quantities of gold and glass beads were also recovered here: the richest burial yielded about 2.2 kilograms of gold.

It was then that the four Afrikaner explorers set in motion a chain of discoveries that challenged the known prehistory of southern Africa.

The adventure seekers had discovered the hidden treasure, but now found themselves in a dangerous situation: they were trespassing and in possession of property which, in the eyes of the law, was stolen. After much debate, they eventually decided to share the gold among themselves.

Fortunately the Van Graans were educated men, with the younger having studied at the University of Pretoria (formerly known as the Transvaal University College). He remembered attending a lecture on the fate of Great Zimbabwe's treasures, a place where no human remains were found and the origins of which had been bitterly disputed for about half a century.

Here at Mapungubwe, they had found what looked like Great Zimbabwe gold, as well as a skeleton. Jerry, riddled with guilt and realising the scientific importance of their discovery, placed a few pieces of gold plate, nails, and some beads in an envelope, and mailed it by registered post to his former professor.

The receipt of these items opened the first chapter of the University of Pretoria's 70-year involvement on this significant site.

The University of Pretoria's role

This discovery coincided with the excavations at Great Zimbabwe, and it was clear that the finds were of great importance and that every effort should be made to recover the entire contents of the burial sites before the graves were looted and lost to 'treasure-seeker' science.

Upon receipt of the envelope, Professor Leo Fouché, head of the Department of History at the University of Pretoria, immediately set about organising an expedition to recover and secure the newly found treasures and surrounding environment for archaeological research.

The university decided to pay the discoverers half the intrinsic metal value of what had been removed and half of the value of whatever else would be excavated. The discoverers agreed, and handed over their finds for valuation purposes, legally ceding all rights to the University of Pretoria.

ABOVE *Among the beads unearthed at Mapungubwe were cobalt-blue glass 'hoop' beads that resemble tiny car tyres.*

ABOVE Hundreds of ceramic pots from Mapungubwe and K2 were painstakingly documented and then restored.

Rumours were also doing the rounds that Mapungubwe gold was being sold illegally in Messina (now Musina), which led to temporary police protection of the site to prevent any illegal removal of artefacts. Apparently, gold beads from Mapungubwe were being sold in jam jars, and three pots of Mapungubwe gold had been melted down, and made into trinkets.

Furthermore, there were – and still are – rumours of gold in private collections and decorating family mantelpieces, and of ceramic pots, strands of trade beads and other artefacts appropriated by treasure seekers, each privately wanting to have their share of the Mapungubwe treasures.

It is an undisputed fact that the university's collection today constitutes a mere fraction of what was originally there centuries years ago.

Mapungubwe was instantly regarded as a Site of National Importance, and the discovery received widespread publicity in the media. Because of Professor Fouché's intervention in June 1933, the government entered into negotiations to buy the farm Greefswald from the property owner, a Witwatersrand attorney by the name of EE Collins. Collins neither lived on the farm nor knew it well, and subsequently sold the land for about 25 pence a morgen.

In accordance with the request of a commission representing the University of Pretoria and the University of the Witwatersrand, the government of the Union of South Africa passed the Act for the Preservation of Ancient Monuments in 1934. This Act created the Government Bureau of Archaeology at the University of the Witwatersrand, where the director, Professor C van Riet Lowe, was involved from the inception of the project.

During the same year, the Archaeological Committee was constituted at the University of Pretoria, which also successfully requested the postponement of any prospecting or mining activities in the region.

A dearth of professional archaeologists, and the absence of an archaeology department at the University of Pretoria, hampered research between 1933 and 1940. Nonetheless, large-scale excavations resulted in the recovery of all the gold and valuable artefacts currently in the Mapungubwe Collection.

The University of Pretoria thus undertook the longest Iron Age archaeological excavation project ever to take place in southern Africa, which in turn had a ripple effect on the shape of the history of South Africa in general.

Mapungubwe had come to the attention of the national and international community as a result of treasure hunters and the secrets of popular legend. Now followed the arrival of scientific researchers with a scientific mission.

ABOVE Mapungubwe's glass beads indicate contact with India, Egypt, Persia and Arabia via the East Coast trade networks.

Archaeological research

Despite much criticism of excavation techniques, recording methods, inadequate funding, poor telegraph communication, absence of stratigraphic records and lack of professional archaeologists, these excavations resulted in the recovery of the gold

Mapungubwe National Park and World Heritage Site

The first step to create this new national park was taken as far back as 1994, with the first negotiations between the then Northern Province and SANParks. The vision also provided the creation of a transfrontier park between South Africa, Botswana and Zimbabwe; Mapungubwe was thus transferred to SANParks as the main core area of the new national park. The site is already a cultural showpiece of the Limpopo-Shashe Transfrontier Conservation Area, of which the Peace Parks Foundation is a major partner. This conservancy, with its unique natural aspects and scenic beauty, offers the visitor endless attractions as the landscape hosts an abundance of San rock paintings, bird life, animal species – including leopard, lion and elephant – and an array of indigenous trees. The park is also home to the 'small five': the rhino beetle, buffalo weaver, elephant shrew, leopard tortoise and lion ant.

The route to Mapungubwe meanders past vast expanses of untamed bushveld, surrounded by some of the finest examples of ancient baobab trees. It is envisaged that Mapungubwe will become a leading example in conservancy and in protecting South Africa's rich cultural heritage.

Jan Smuts: Mapungubwe's visionary

Interestingly enough, the vision of this conservancy area originated in the early 1920s, when protecting the wildlife of the area, and Mapungubwe in turn, was the initiative of General Jan Smuts. Smuts, perhaps better known as a statesman and politician, spent much of his spare time exploring the natural world of South Africa. Botanist, philosopher and lover of nature, his endeavours for attempting to preserve South Africa's heritage should not go unnoticed.

In 1922, he arranged that a block of nine farms, of which Greefswald was one, be set aside as the Dongola Botanical Reserve, the aim of which was to protect and preserve the natural vegetation, wildlife and objects of ethnological, historical or scientific interest. The Welsh botanist Dr Illtyd Buller Pole-Evans, together with Prime Minister Smuts and Conroy (then Minister of Lands) had come to the conclusion that the land was unfit for human settlement, and that saving the land from further ruin would necessitate the formation of a 'Wildlife Sanctuary' for the nation.

The possibility of linking the sanctuary with conservation areas in the neighbouring countries of Botswana and Zimbabwe was also considered. The concept was hotly debated in Parliament and in the press, to the extent that it became known as the 'Battle of Dongola'.

ABOVE Some of the original stone walling found on Mapungubwe Hill is no longer visible today as it is now covered with deep archaeological deposits that formed part of the early excavations.

It also became the subject of party political rancour, with Smuts's government in favour of the reserve, and the opposition against it. Despite the controversy, the Dongola Wild Life Sanctuary Act No. 6 of 1947 was passed, proclaiming an area of 190 000 hectares near Pontdrift. The act was repealed within a year following the National Party's coming to power in the 1948 election. This was the first Act to be repealed in the new Parliament. Donors were refunded and farms returned to their previous owners.

The Dongola Botanical Reserve was abolished and allocated for settlement by white farmers. If, in a dream world, Smuts and Pole-Evans had in fact succeeded in establishing the conservancy area of Mapungubwe, the need to protect the cultural and ecological biodiversity of Mapungubwe would have been a battle already won.

The cultural landscape

Mapungubwe was indeed inhabited before the advent of Iron. Dinosaurs roamed the Limpopo Valley; there are dinosaur footprints near Pontdrift, and the sleeping dinosaur fossil of *Massospondylus carinatus* lies lazily in the stone formations not far from Mapungubwe Hill itself.

However, it was the nomadic hunter-gatherers who purposefully chose and fashioned the distinct white concretions of calcite and quartz into stone tools, as the concoidal fractures of these pebbles make suitably sharp blades. For 5 000 years, these Later Stone Age peoples roamed the river flood plains and cave sandstone hills of the Limpopo Valle, and the San hunter-gatherers also

copper ingot

ABOVE *General Jan Smuts visited Mapungubwe in July 1934. Standing on the Southern Terrace are, from left to right, Professor C van Riet Lowe, General Smuts and Reverend Neville Jones.*

left their legacies in the form of paintings and engravings in stone. The Limpopo-Shashe confluence area is rich in paintings, with more than 150 documented rock-art sites and over 450 previously unknown sites. Depictions of grasshoppers, unique to the Limpopo Valley, and paintings of V-shaped figures, probably depicting loincloths, adorn the rock shelters. Rock engravings show an array of sable antelope, hippo and elephant, the Mapungubwe rocks forming the perfect painter's canvas.

There is no doubt that the Mapungubwe cultural landscape, which is representative of the Stone Age, Iron Age and the Historical period, is an archaeologist's playground. Here the richness of the cultural remains from these sites and the surrounding Limpopo Valley surpasses that of most of the contemporary settlements in southern Africa.

The first settlement of Europeans in the Soutpansberg district during the nineteenth century, and the seasonal presence of the tsetse fly in the Transvaal

ABOVE *A young woman at a local Venda village situated near Musina in 1934.*

ABOVE *A number of archival photographs record some of the ceramics excavated from Mapungubwe Hill.*

Lowveld, made cattle herding difficult for the local Iron Age communities. Malaria added to the difficult conditions. As the Mapungubwe region became unfit for habitation, it was used as hunting grounds and for forestry and mining activities. Prospectors and treasure seekers were attracted to the area, which eventually led to the discovery of gold.

According to oral tradition, communities such as the Venda, Shona and Sotho-speaking people settled in the region only after AD 1700. There, is in, fact no substantial evidence of who lived at Mapungubwe, as the evidence is largely archaeological and no oral tradition could stand testimony over 1000 years. For this very reason, no one really knows the origins and language of the 'Mapungubweans', or where exactly they went, but they produced some of the finest gold artwork found on the African continent.

The archaeological sites

The Mapungubwe site was inhabited during the Late Iron Age, from about AD 970 to AD 1290, and is believed to have been the centre of the first kingdom in southern Africa. The site consists of three living areas: first, there is the Mapungubwe hilltop, which sports a healthy layer of soil and vegetation, and is believed to have been a little more than barren rock in its mid-Jurassic period about 175 million years ago. The second living area is the Southern Terrace at the foot of the hill, and the third, K2, a valley southwest of Bambandyanalo Hill. K2 was inhabited from around AD 970 for about 100 years. The occupation then shifted to the other side of Bambandyanalo, to the Southern Terrace of Mapungubwe Hill. Here the commoners lived at the foot of Mapungubwe Hill, while royalty resided at the summit from AD 1220 to AD 1290 – a mere 70-year period.

A wide valley surrounds Mapungubwe Hill on every side, where it is flanked in the south by a small hill known as Mapungubanyana (also known as Little Muck or 'Little Mapungubwe'). Around AD 970, K2, Mapungubwe Hill and the Southern Terrace were simultaneously inhabited. K2 was abandoned 40 years later and settlement took place at Mapungubwe Hill, where a royal kingdom was established early in AD 1200. From the quantity of cultural material and the sheer size of the Mapungubwe kingdom, it is assumed that the royalty reigned over a very large population, estimated to be close to 9 000 people. A population of this size at that time suggests a region about the size of KwaZulu-Natal.

A substantial archaeological deposit, characterised by a vertical succession of gravel floors, the rubble of burnt huts, some small rough stone platforms and grindstones, covers the crest of Mapungubwe Hill. Terrace walling and isolated, freestanding stone walls do occur on the hill. Potsherds, animal bones, metal fragments, mortar and pounding stones, glass trade beads and over 100 human burial sites lay scattered across the bushveld.

Eight of the graves held adult remains while four held juveniles. Only three of the graves contained gold. Another 15 skeletons were discovered on the hill, but these were either fragmentary or have since disintegrated. These burials were all located in a single cemetery, indicating that the individuals may represent a single family, or may have been a socially distinct group, such as a royal bloodline.

Mapungubwe Hill's main entrance is the Western Ascent, which lies on the Southern Terrace and is generally used as a means of reaching the summit. Initially, there was an entrance to the summit known as the Eastern Ascent, but this has collapsed and is

ABOVE *Part of the early diggings included a stone platform excavated on the Southern Terrace.*

no longer usable. Today, an inconspicuous staircase provides access to the Eastern Ascent.

There is another ascent called Mahobi's, on the southern side of Mapungubwe Hill, directly below a cliff face. Legend has it that Mahobi, a daughter of Mapungubwe, resided on this side of the hill, but there is no evidence to support this. The Southern Terrace stretches along the entire length of the base of the southern side of Mapungubwe Hill.

The remains of rough stone walls and steps meander between large boulders, which form an entrance. The deposit, similar to that of Mapungubwe Hill, yet without any human burials, is remarkably deep, slightly elevating this commoner settlement off the valley floor.

K2, named after the successive settlements known as Koms (similar to the Tells of the Near East) in North Africa, lies in a small valley surrounded by sandstone cliffs. This settlement appears as an open grass-covered area, and is immediately recognisable by the huge centrally located ash midden about 6 metres deep. The pale deposit is mixed with fine-grained sand and small quantities of potsherds, bones and charcoal.

The K2 site consists of a central kraal area, which overlaps with the huge midden surrounded by peripheral homesteads. The architecture of the K2 people was limited to simple pole and daga huts. Hut poles were relatively thin and covered with a sandy plaster.

The domestic area, to the east on a rocky ridge, consists of stratified mudstone gravel floors and large double-walled and medium-sized huts, clustered closely together around smaller grain storage huts (granary bins) and midden remains.

The eastern midden, known as K1, lies on the lower level of the valley. Ninety-seven skeletons have been excavated at K2; burials are situated in the living area, in ash heaps and in the central kraal area. Generally, unimportant people were buried in middens; the chief might have been buried in the cattle kraal, while some members of the family were buried under the floor of the hut or just behind the hut.

ABOVE *Captain Guy Attwater Gardner, excavating in 1935, remains one of the unsung heroes of Mapungubwe.*

ABOVE *Some of the trenches excavated on Mapungubwe Hill revealed complete or near-complete pottery.*

The human remains at K2 comprised 76 children as well as a few adult males and females. A complete infant was found buried with glass beads. An unusual burial was discovered near K2 where the remains of an elderly male were found inside a pot.

Most of the human burials were found in flexed or foetal positions, generally lying on their right side, although some were lying on their left side. Others were found in an upright or sitting position.

Most of the burials contained funerary ware or burial artefacts such as glass beads, ostrich eggshell beads, iron, copper, ivory, animal bones, pots and bone implements. Only in the case of the royal burials on the hill were vast quantities of gold buried with the deceased.

ABOVE *The journey of discovery in the early days of excavation revealed great treasures beyond most archaeologists' wildest dreams. Among the exciting finds were animal bones, meticulously unearthed by pioneer explorers at Mapungubwe.*

the traditional Venda custom of burying a domestic animal when a family member dies away from home, and it is not possible to bring the body back to the homestead. Despite the countless interpretations and possible religious ideas associated with bulls across the African continent, there is no doubt that these 'Beast Burials' are undeniably one of the most important and baffling discoveries at Mapungubwe.

Excavations have uncovered proof of Mapungubwe as our first kingdom, which grew and flourished because of wealth accumulated from trade in gold, glass beads, cotton cloth, Chinese and local ceramics, ivory, copper,

ABOVE *An archival portrait dating back to 1934 of John, a Lemba custodian of the Dongola Botanical Reserve.*

To the east of K2 lies a huge flat-topped hill known as Bambandyanalo. From this hill comes the evidence of an advanced culture based on the ownership of livestock. It seems occupation shifted from K2 and Bambandyanalo to Mapungubwe Hill and the Southern Terrace when the village became overpopulated. It was during this time that royalty resided on the hill.

Six rather bizarre graves, known as the 'Beast Burials', contained cattle bones, which were buried with layers of potsherds, spouted pots, copper bangles, land snail shells, cowries, glass beads, dismembered bones of rodents and pigs, and even good-quality mica placed inside bracelets. When reconstructed, the ceramic sherds reconstituted 14 pots. Nowhere else on either K2 or Mapungubwe were pieces of mica found.

These cattle burials have been associated with the bull cults of ancient Egypt. Another suggested explanation for the burials is that they are related to and hides with the Indian Ocean network and the Swahili merchants on the East Coast of Africa.

The deep depression on the summit made it possible to remove layer after layer of history trapped in the soil, providing clues as to when the ancestors of the Bantu-speaking people first crossed the Limpopo River, and also preserving the remains of the intricately wrought gold artefacts, for which Mapungubwe is now famous.

Traditional ways of life

Stone walls and terrace farming covered the slopes and homesteads were scattered about, with royalty living naturally protected at the top of Mapungubwe Hill, and supported by the commoners in the valley. K2 indicated that these inhabitants were subsistence farmers, practicing mixed agriculture and pastoralism.

Some people were prosperous and kept domesticated cattle, sheep and goats; hunting, snaring and fishing was not the basis of their existence. The charred remains of storage huts, grinding stones, iron hoes and spindle whorls have also been found, and there is evidence that pearl millet, sorghum, several species of bean and cotton were also cultivated.

When the Mapungubweans moved to the hill, their lifestyle focused more on extensive trade and technology, and smiths created objects of iron, bronze, copper and gold for practical and decorative purposes, both for local use and for trade.

The nature of society had changed, so political and social interactions became more complex.

Through the East Coast trade, the accumulation of wealth was inevitable. Large quantities of finished bone tools such as needles, hairpins, awls and link shafts are also part of the collection, but may not indicate a specialised bone craft.

ABOVE *Of the many archaeological deposits that now form part of the landscape at Mapungubwe Hill, the deepest is that of K8, which is situated on the Southern Terrace. The deposit is approximately 3.5 metres in depth.*

Beads

Glass beads were valued, and still are throughout Africa, not because people were fooled into believing them to be precious stones, but because they were the products of an exotic technology, the equivalent of which was unknown in Africa at that time.

Beads became precious in their own right, and were soon linked to whatever was valued in the cultures of the people who owned and crafted them into a variety of objects to be worn according to custom, as tokens of social status, political importance and for personal adornment.

The presence of countless beads can chronicle substantial information about the nature of the society that wore them. Thousands of glass beads, together with flat circles of ostrich-egg and land-snail (*Achatina immaculate*) shell beads, gold and copper beads have been found in abundance in the middens and graves at K2 and Mapungubwe.

From the presence of glass beads left in the archaeological record, these minute creations play an important role in the accumulation of wealth by those merchants controlling trade. Beads are not easily destroyed and they are easy to transport. Glass beads originated in the Middle East about 4 500 years ago – long before the Christian era – where they were part of sea trade during the Bronze era. It is from the Middle East that the technology spread.

ABOVE This finely crafted gold necklace is draped around the neck of a large wide-bellied pot unearthed from Mapungubwe Hill. The pot has a series of incised diamond- and triangle-shaped decorations that are typical of pottery found at Mapungubwe.

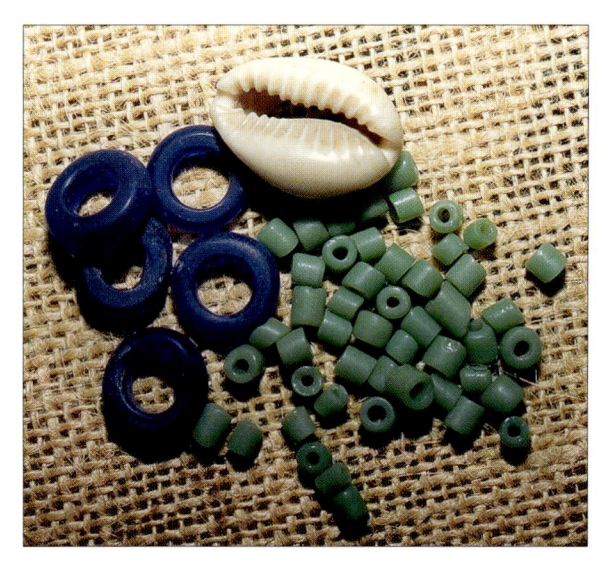

ABOVE Many trade glass beads and cowry shells were excavated from both K2 and Mapungubwe Hill.

China was producing glass beads by around 1 000 BC and the glass bead tradition spread rather slowly reaching India by at least the third century BC.

But how did the beads end up in the Limpopo Valley, so far down south? This is a perplexing question, but the general theory is that trade relations reached eastern and southern Africa by sea. The route from the Red Sea southwards passed many trading ports known to the captains of the dhows which sailed from Arabia, Egypt and even Cambay, north of Bombay in India, to various ancient trading ports such as Kilwa, Sofala and Chibuene, via Madagascar, and back up the east coast with the seasonal monsoon winds.

Some of the beads are known as 'trade wind beads', 'Indian red' or 'cambay' beads and others are known as 'seed beads' due to the miniscule size. The origins of all the beads remain obscure, but the beads found in the Limpopo Valley are thought to originate from India, Egypt (Fustat – Old Cairo), Southeast Asia, and the Middle East.

There are also the hexagonal royal blue glass beads that resemble tiny motorcar tyres, which were found at Mapungubwe and were still traded less than a hundred years ago. In the 1900s, a Rhodesian farmer was told by one of his workers that each of the Mapungubwe blue beads was worth £5, and would buy one cow.

The descriptions of these glass beads are endless. However, the most interesting of all the beads is the indigenous 'home-grown' or rather reworked glass beads found at K2. The K2 people locally manufactured these large beads, known as 'garden roller beads' (named after the shape of iron rollers used to surface English lawns). Whole and broken turquoise trade beads were melted and the molten glass was wound into a prefabricated clay mould to set. The clay mould was then broken to remove the new garden roller bead.

The technology used to make 'garden rollers' is unique, as nowhere else in Africa are single clay moulds used to make beads. K2, therefore, stands as the earliest instance of glass reworking in Africa.

However, these large barrel-shaped glass beads were not extensively traded, and are found in small numbers in limited areas only in southern Africa.

Apart from the 'garden rollers', the sheer volume of glass beads recovered from the Mapungubwe graves is astonishing. In one instance, a ceramic pot was found in a nearby cave, filled to the brim with glass beads. As one early excavator put it 'beads form an appreciable volume … as indeed the quantity of

ABOVE Black glass trade beads originating from Egypt were commonly found in burials.

beads to be recovered depends entirely on the patience of the collector.'

Shells such as the cowrie and ostrich egg were also modified into beads. The most interesting, however, is the presence of the terrestrial land snail. These shells were found predominantly at K2 and show signs of cultural modifications interpreted by the apex of the shell being cut away.

They may have carried religious significance, as they were often used as grave goods, even in the 'Beast Burials'. The cowrie shell is one of the most primitive currencies and was used before the advent of gold and silver coinage. This shell extended its range further than any form of money before or since, spreading from China and India to the Pacific Islands, travelling across and around Africa and even penetrating the New World. These shells are believed to have occult or supernatural powers and are used in divination, traditional medicine, fertility practices, ancestor worship and rituals.

The cowrie once highlighted some aspects of Africa's evolutionary path; it is a pity it was stopped short by the invention of coinage.

Ceramicware

The accumulation of gold and glass trade beads substantially contributed to the wealth and status of the inhabitants at Mapungubwe, bringing about social, political and religious stratifications. The social division between royalty living on Mapungubwe Hill and the commoners in the valley is also echoed by the varieties of ceramicware and other crafts, such as clay figurines and spindle whorls.

Pottery, in all probability, originated among people who were practising some form of agriculture. Hunter-gatherer communities seldom stayed in a place long enough to make ceramics, and vessels were, for practical purposes, made of skins instead of material susceptible to breaking. After all, at Mapungubwe the ceramics and agricultural activities were attributed to labour by women and part of pot-making is the traditional knowledge of the soil, as the selection of clay determines its texture, shaping and firing.

It is no wonder that ceramics are very common at most archaeological sites; yet, because of this very familiarity, they tend to be neglected. Keep in mind that it is the lone decorated potsherd that is the key to revealing that part of the history of Mapungubwe which precedes recorded history.

Preserved in the middens, being practically indestructible and available in vast quantities, ceramic sherds have provided details to the Mapungubweans' rise, contact, wanderings and decline. The typical pot decoration of diagonally incised triangles was, in fact, the 'trademark' of this thriving community.

K2 spouted pot

Tracing the decorations on sherds and distributions, one can tell a story of human progress and deterioration. With hundreds of decorative variations, the ceramics are characterised by incised, geometric patterns with cross-hatching and parallel grooving etched into the wet clay. The ceramic beakers, shallow bowls, spouted pots, and deep pots made from either fine, course or burnished clay come in a variety of shapes and sizes, all made by hand and only by

ABOVE Among the finds taken from the K2 site in 1935 were ivory bands, which were used as bracelets.

women. Drinking cups, storage containers, cooking pots, shallow bowls for grain, from pint-sized to large enough for someone to be cooked in, make up a collection of over 450 vessels, not all complete.

Clay figurines

Figurines fired from clay and representing stylised humans, animals and conical objects have been recovered from sites throughout southern Africa and have been associated with the female form or fertility.

Most of the ceramic figurines were found at K2. Human figurines were usually made up of an elongated body with stumps for heads, arms and legs. Many depict the female figure by small protuberances for breasts. Other characteristics include a protruding navel (umbilical hernia), and torsos impressed or incised with decorative

ABOVE *From evidence gleaned from the Mapungubwe site, clay was commonly sculpted to create stylised human figurines. Typically, lumps tended to depict rounded human heads, buttocks and breasts.*

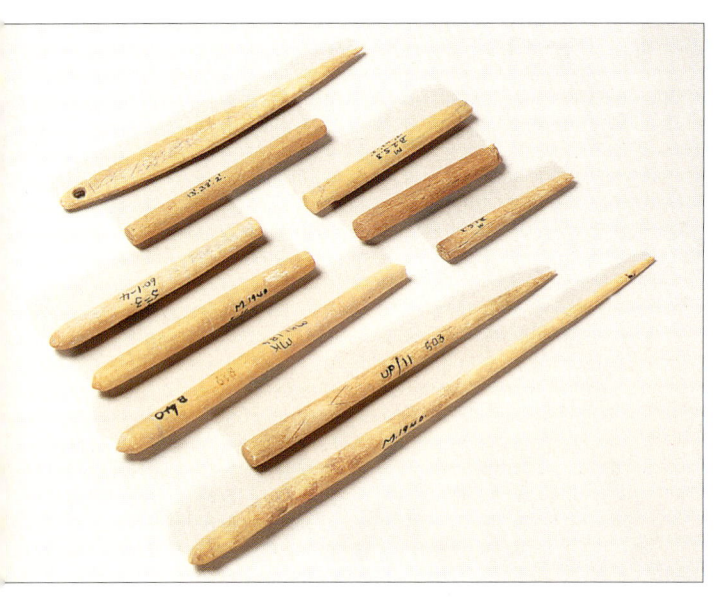

ABOVE *Animal bone was refined and meticulously fashioned into needles, awls and points.*

distinctive patterns on the back, sides and around the navel, possibly reminiscent of the scarification marks on the female inhabitants themselves.

Clay animal figurines such as cattle, goats and sheep probably depict the domestic animals kept by the people at Mapungubwe. Many of the cattle figurines are modelled with precision – to such a degree that even the udders of cows and goats and even the dewlaps of cattle are very clearly depicted. Some figurines clearly display a pronounced hump behind the head, which is indicative of the so-called Sanga cattle of Africa.

Sheep figurines are rare, yet are just as fascinating as the other domestic animals. The rear of an ewe apparently has a very distinctive shape, and many of the sheep figurines depict no tail, indicating that these Iron Age communities may have practised tail docking. Many of the animal figurines were the work of adults, and may have had some significance in the social structure beyond that of a mere child's toy.

The most remarkable figurines are those of wild animals, such as a small ceramic giraffe, with its curled tail held above the rump, a position that it would hold while running, and a perfectly proportioned, elongated neck. The rarest figurine in the collection is that of a stylised hippopotamus with a human torso and green trade bead eyes pushed into the clay, found at K2.

Such figurines and other conical-shaped figurines, or phallic symbols, are thought to be associated with male and female initiation ceremonies, where they were used to demonstrate points of instruction, and illustrate life skills, histories and traditions.

human clay figurine

ABOVE *Whereas Mapungubwe revealed a number of fascinating finds, it is the gold that remains the most intriguing in public consciousness. Gold ornaments and gold beads, AD 1220–1290, were taken from the royal burial cemetery on Mapungubwe's summit.*

Some practical everyday ceramic items include miniature bowls, spoons, whistles, clay stoppers, and clay earplugs. Small flat doughnut-shaped spindle whorls from Mapungubwe and K2 were fashioned from either ceramic or stone; some were even decorated by drawing incisions into the wet clay and were used to spin cotton.

The resulting thread would then have been woven into a textile of some sort. This slow, painstaking process requiring specialised skills was probably a craft practised solely by women. The spindle whorls at Mapungubwe are the earliest evidence for a weaving industry and even woven basket fragments were unearthed from excavations.

Ivory and bone

Next to gold, ivory was the most sought-after precious product from Africa, and elephant ivory was one of the strongest motives for the development of Arab trade with the southern African interior.

There is evidence of a thriving local trade in worked ivory at K2. People were probably bringing in raw ivory where the tusk was split into plates of a certain thickness before being smoothed off to make an armband. One of the most interesting ivory finds at K2 was a decorated ivory armband, which was possibly used to protect the wrist against the backlash of the bowstring when hunting.

Other artefacts of animal origin, such as hundreds of bone points, awls and flat needles, were used in the manufacturing and sewing of animal skins. Some of the inhabitants of Mapungubwe made and used polished bone arrowheads and bone link shafts, similar to the arrows used by the San or Bushmen.

Some bone arrowheads have flattened front ends into which iron tips were fitted and were possibly even dipped into poison to bring the animal down. The sheer quantity of these finely finished bone points is unique in southern Africa and the large quantities suggest a surplus, which may have been manufactured solely for trade.

Gold

Referred to as South Africa's crown jewels, Mapungubwe's gold is legendary in its own right.

Mapungubwe Hill represents the earliest known recorded archaeological gold in southern Africa. Here, all that glitters is gold; three royal burials entombed for seven centuries captured the imaginations not only of the treasure hunters who sought the gold.

Mapungubwe's gold reflects a great beauty and a remarkable technical sophistication, where pure gold was more valued for its social purpose of adornment or ritual, rather than its economic value.

Found along with these skeletal remains were gold wire anklets, gold beads and nails. One burial alone contained over 2.2 kilograms of gold and over 12 000 gold beads. Two of these individuals were buried in a sitting position, indicative of high social status in southern Africa, while the rest were buried in flexed positions on their sides, knees drawn up to the chest, with their heads facing east, in keeping with the tradition of facing in the direction of one's origin.

decorated gold orament

Near one of the skulls were remains of gold sheathing from a wooden headrest. In another grave, a gold staff of office and fragments of a gold rhinoceros were found. Gold had been fashioned into ornaments or sacred animals from fine gold sheeting

ABOVE Archival photographs taken during the early excavations show tattooing on the torsos of local BaLemba girls.

or foil that was hammered, engraved, coiled, and pierced along the edges or seams and then mounted onto wood. Some gold was tacked with minute gold nails to wooden objects, which have long since decayed. Gold beads were drawn or cast, and some of the gold was drawn into wire, wound and used in decorative heliacal 'braiding' as anklets, bangles and necklace ornaments.

The proliferation of precious objects found in these graves was attributed to high-ranking members of royalty, perhaps the head of the Mapungubwe Empire, an elder's organisation, or adviser's political status, which may counterbalance royal power. The adornments of royalty correspond with their responsibilities and leaders used their royal regalia to verify their rights to succession and to legitimise their positions. Members of the royal court sometimes had exclusive rights to certain materials and technologies; perhaps this is the reason why gold artefacts were limited to Mapungubwe Hill.

Other grave articles such as ceramicware, copper, iron, land-snail shells, ostrich eggshells and trade glass beads were used as funerary decorations. Some of the ceramicware and gold ornaments from Mapungubwe Hill show great attention to detail, where the artists of this kingdom used sophisticated technologies to create objects in which rich surface patterns and textures have, perhaps, complex meanings.

The gold ornaments from Mapungubwe Hill were probably used as insignia of office, where the objects in question made a person's political and religious hierarchies apparent.

The gold rhinoceros

The most famous of the gold artefacts recovered from Mapungubwe Hill is undoubtedly the short-legged, one-horned gold rhinoceros. This 'big five' figurine is a unique and magnificent piece of craftsmanship, with sturdy shoulders and two additional rounded gold nails for eyes. The upright tail is a solid, thin cylinder tapering towards the tip and has several engraved marks for decoration, giving the impression of a switch. The two tubular ears, which look more like a kudu's ears, are separately attached and held in position on the head by a small gold nail tacked deep inside each ear. The rounded, rather fat belly is shaped out of two finely beaten sheets of gold foil only 0.5 millimetres thick. The rhino was originally formed onto a wooden core and held in place with minute gold nails. The single horn is a cone of gold plate, fixed below the eyes to the head, which is in a grazing position. It could be a white, black or perhaps a one-horned Sumatran rhinoceros, but is the only existing gold rhinoceros in the world.

However, this rhinoceros is not alone as there are two other animal torsos in the collection. Unfortunately, these are not as complete and have not been restored. Among these remains is also thought to be the remains of the legendary gold buffalo from Mapungubwe.

ABOVE This photograph of Chief Tshirundu from Shirbeek is one of many taken in 1937 of all known chiefs in the vicinity.

The decline of Mapungubwe

A significant discovery was that the Mapungubweans consumed domestic livestock rather than wild game. With the southern Bantu-speaking groups, this was seldom the case; instead, together with gold, livestock represents a form of wealth. But pastoral and agricultural communities need land to sustain them. With the onset of the Little Ice Age in the 13th century, environmental attrition may have caused the demise of Mapungubwe. One theory is that by AD 1300, the Limpopo Valley suffered the worst drought in 15 000 years, which may have precipitated Mapungubwe's end, forcing the community to seek fertile soil elsewhere.

No evidence points to massacre, tribal invasions, or a forced movement further down south in search of greener pastures. Another theory points to a possible outbreak of a plague, carried by domestic rats (*Rattus rattus*), brought in by trade merchants from the East Coast, which may have further blighted the last days of Mapungubwe. Alternatively, it is assumed that as a result of a severe drought brought on by the small Ice Age, Mapungubwe was unable to support its people, and the ruler's inability to supply and trade in ivory, gold, and animal skins to the East Coast merchants may have resulted in the decline of this great trading centre. This also might have hastened a change in trade patterns, shifting the regional dominance to Great Zimbabwe, enabling them to take the advantage of the East Coast trade network, and resulting in the powerful rise of the Empire of Monomotapa, which lasted from AD 1300 to AD 1450.

The ecological crisis theory is the most widely accepted, but this, together with the rise to power of Great Zimbabwe, does not give a definite answer as to where the people of Mapungubwe went, why they left, or even just who they were?

ABOVE *This rare photograph from the Mapungubwe Archives was taken in 1934, and reveals the vast quantities of gold in just one burial. Today, this gold is on exhibition at the Mapungubwe Museum.*

Conclusions

Mapungubwe celebrates the irrefutable fact that a southern African kingdom intrinsically grew and flourished long before the colonisation of Africa. It will always remain a mystery; were it not for the discoverers and the many dedicated archaeologists, Mapungubwe, as we know it today, would not exist.

Archaeology, overall, is a sobering field of expertise; it puts the lifetime of an individual in perspective, not only over a thousand years, but since the dawn of humankind. Mapungubwe and its treasured archaeological collection is a gentle reminder of a tremendous contribution not only to the African Renaissance, but also to human progress over millennia on the southern African continent.

Seven decades ago, these great archaeological treasures from a remote area on the southern African continent became known to the world. Then, the discoverers could have had had no inkling of the significance of their find.

Today, almost 10 centuries after the decline of this great civilisation, the legendary Mapungubwe continues, and thrives as a museum at the University of Pretoria, and as a National Park and World Heritage Site.

Pause for a moment on Mapungubwe Hill, or gaze upon the gold rhino. They offer South Africans something of which we can all be justly proud.

circular gold ornament

ABOVE The gold rhinoceros, once a symbol of royalty, lay for seven centuries in a sacred grave on Mapungubwe Hill until it was unearthed in 1933. This is undoubtedly the most famous of gold artefacts found in the southern African archaeological record. Today, its embodies the very spirit of the African Renaissance and also signifies the Order of Mapungubwe, which is awarded for exceptional achievement and excellence. The award's first recipient was Nelson Mandela.

OPPOSITE This fat-bellied rhinoceros is about 15.2 centimetres in length and shaped out of two finely beaten sheets of gold foil only 0.5 millimetres thick, and was fashioned around a soft core, probably sculpted wood, and held in place with minute gold nails. Its single horn is a cone of gold plate centred between two rounded gold nails for eyes. The upright tail is solid and the animal's strength is depicted in short, stubby legs and sturdy shoulders. This figurine – representing one of Africa's 'Big Five' – is a unique and magnificent example of indigenous craftsmanship.

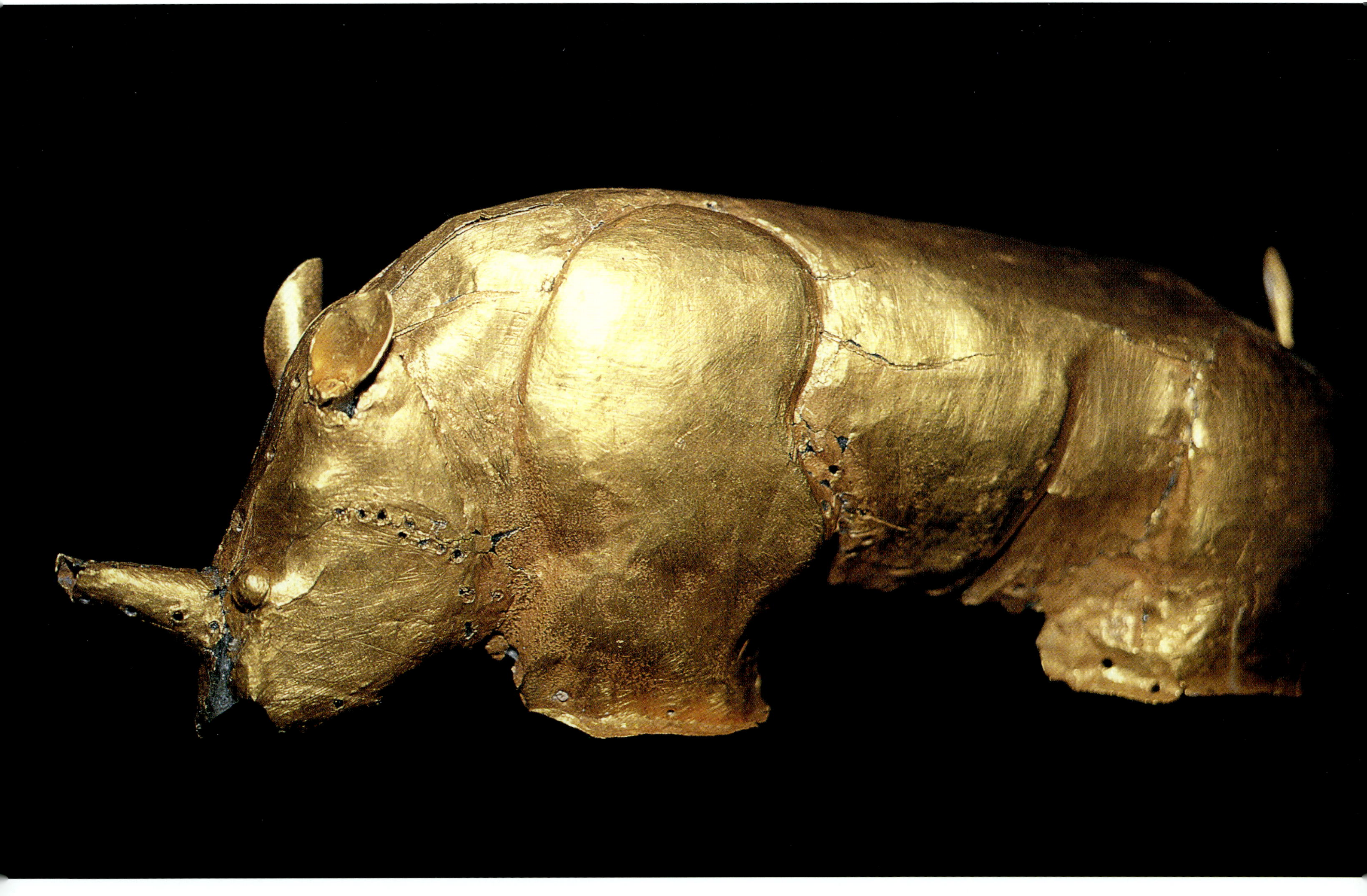

28 MAPUNGUBWE

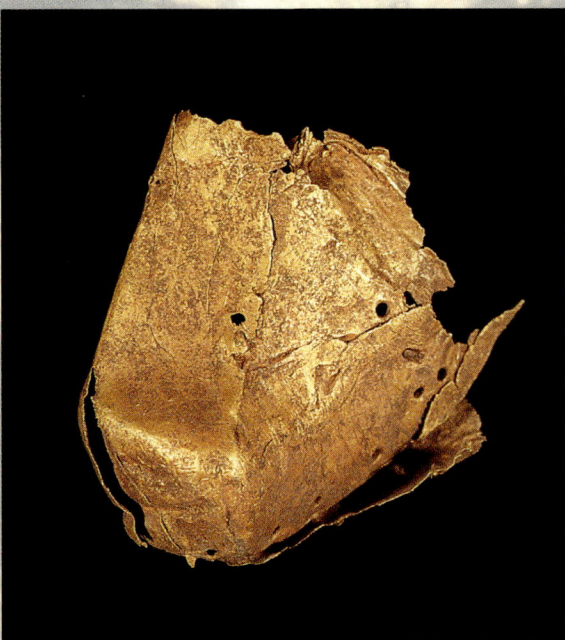

The gold rhinoceros is the only complete and restored animal unearthed at Mapungubwe. However, two other rhino torsos lie among the fragments of torn gold, other ears and tapered solid tails and the remains of the snout of a gold buffalo. These were probably sacred animals made from fine gold foil that was hammered, engraved, coiled, and pierced along the edges or seams and then mounted onto wood. The foil was then tacked with minute gold nails to wooden objects that have long since decayed.
TOP LEFT Tiny gold nails.
LEFT, CENTRE Gold tail.
LEFT, BOTTOM The largest of the gold nails.
ABOVE Snout of a gold buffalo.
TOP RIGHT AND RIGHT Gold funnel shapes, which could possibly be horns.

BELOW AND TOP RIGHT *The remains of an animal torso.*
BOTTOM *The gold tail (bottom) is a solid, thin cylinder that tapers to the tip and has several engraved marks for decoration, giving the impression of a switch. The tubular ears (top) of solid gold, resembling kudu ears, are separately attached and held in position by a small gold nail tacked deep inside the ear.*
RIGHT AND BOTTOM RIGHT *Nails were cut from tapered gold rods and then hammered cold, forming a flattened head.*
BOTTOM CENTRE *Two large gold ears.*

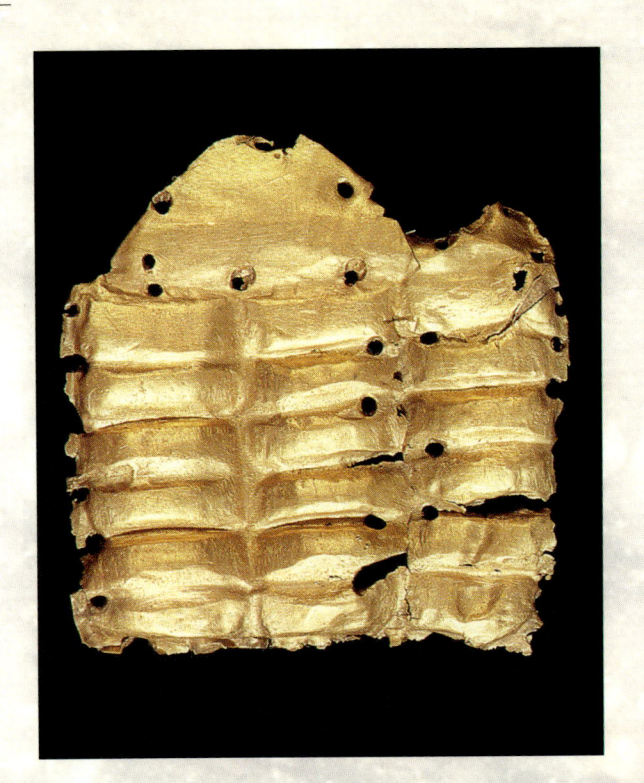

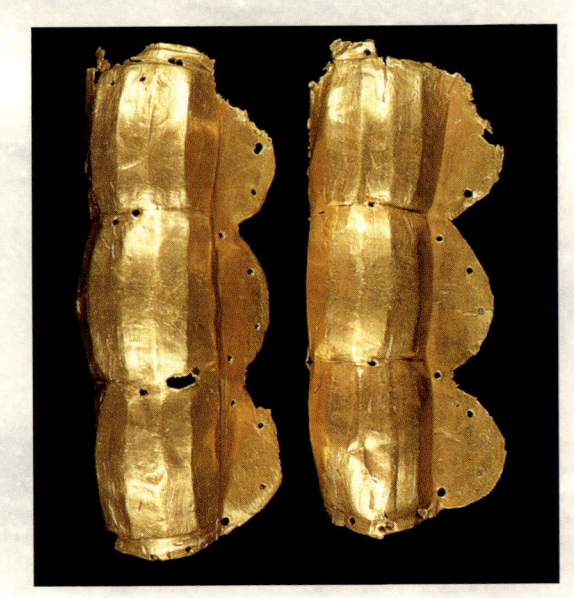

MAPUNGUBWE

The function of these unusual gold-ribbed objects was invariably linked to a symbolic meaning that offers a glimpse into a profound philosophy, a rich spirituality, and the organisation of Mapungubwe society.
OPPOSITE PAGE, TOP RIGHT, BOTTOM LEFT AND RIGHT *Geometric shapes were used frequently and some representations in gold are abstract and do not seem to take a specific form. Many of the gold pieces reveal a deep aesthetic beauty created by goldsmiths as ornaments and jewellery where shape and form are brought together as an deep appreciation of a valuable metal.*
RIGHT *This gold bangle is now in four separate pieces but once covered a wooden bangle that has since disintegrated*

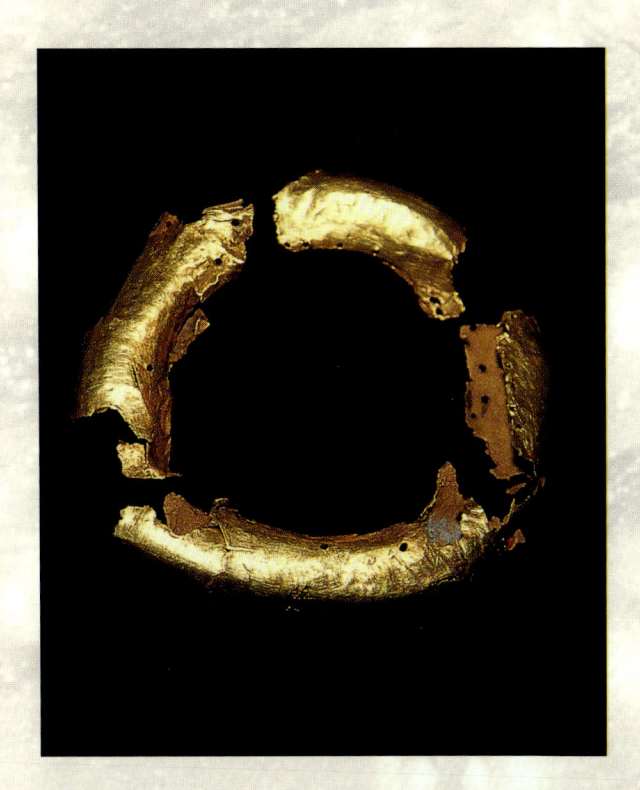

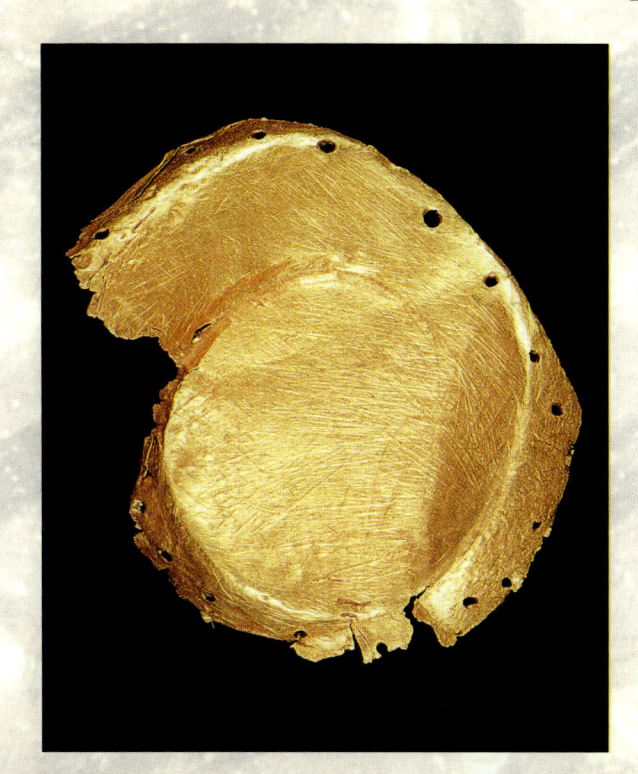

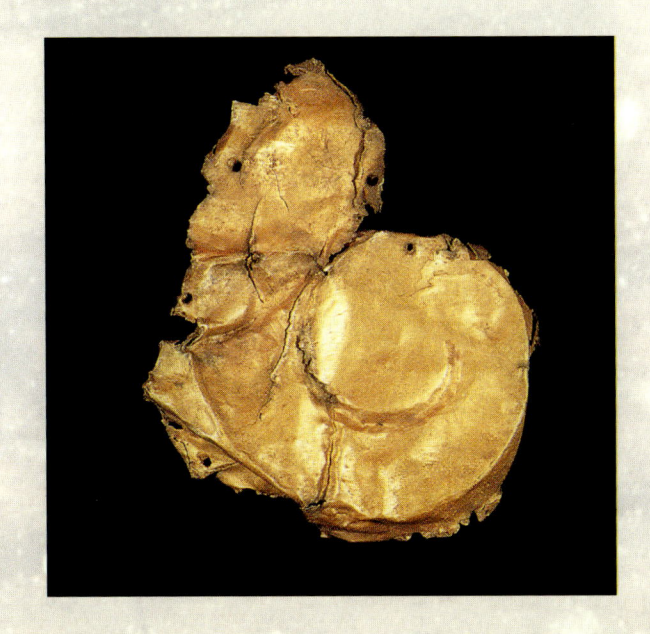

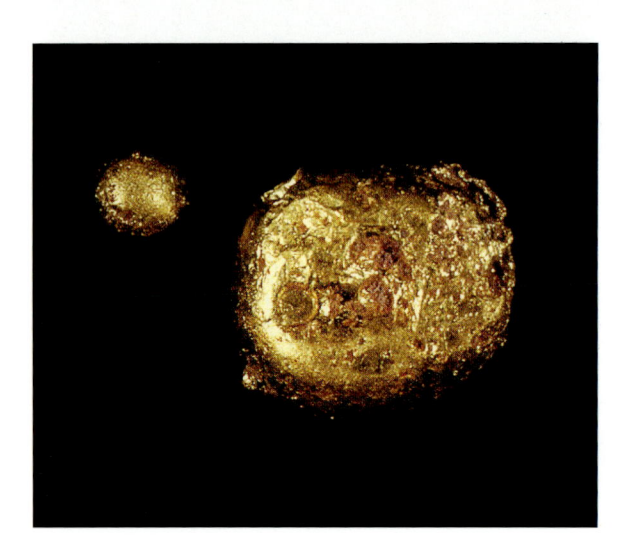

THIS PAGE *The gold fabrication technology is clearly indigenous and no finished objects were cast. Beads were punched from near-spherical gold droplets (depicted here on the left with a smaller gold droplet), probably formed by pouring molten gold into water. These were flattened (top right) using light blows with a small iron hammer and then punched from both sides using a four-sided tapered punch. This produced solid gold beads without a join, but often with the tell-tale marks of the punch preserved around the hole, which has been worn round from being strung onto a necklace, for example.*
OPPOSITE *Gold was one of the most sought-after trade commodities – not only because of its economic value but also because of the symbolic significance attached to this precious metal. Copious amounts of gold beads were excavated from three royal burials on Mapungubwe Hill. No other gold was found in the vicinity.*

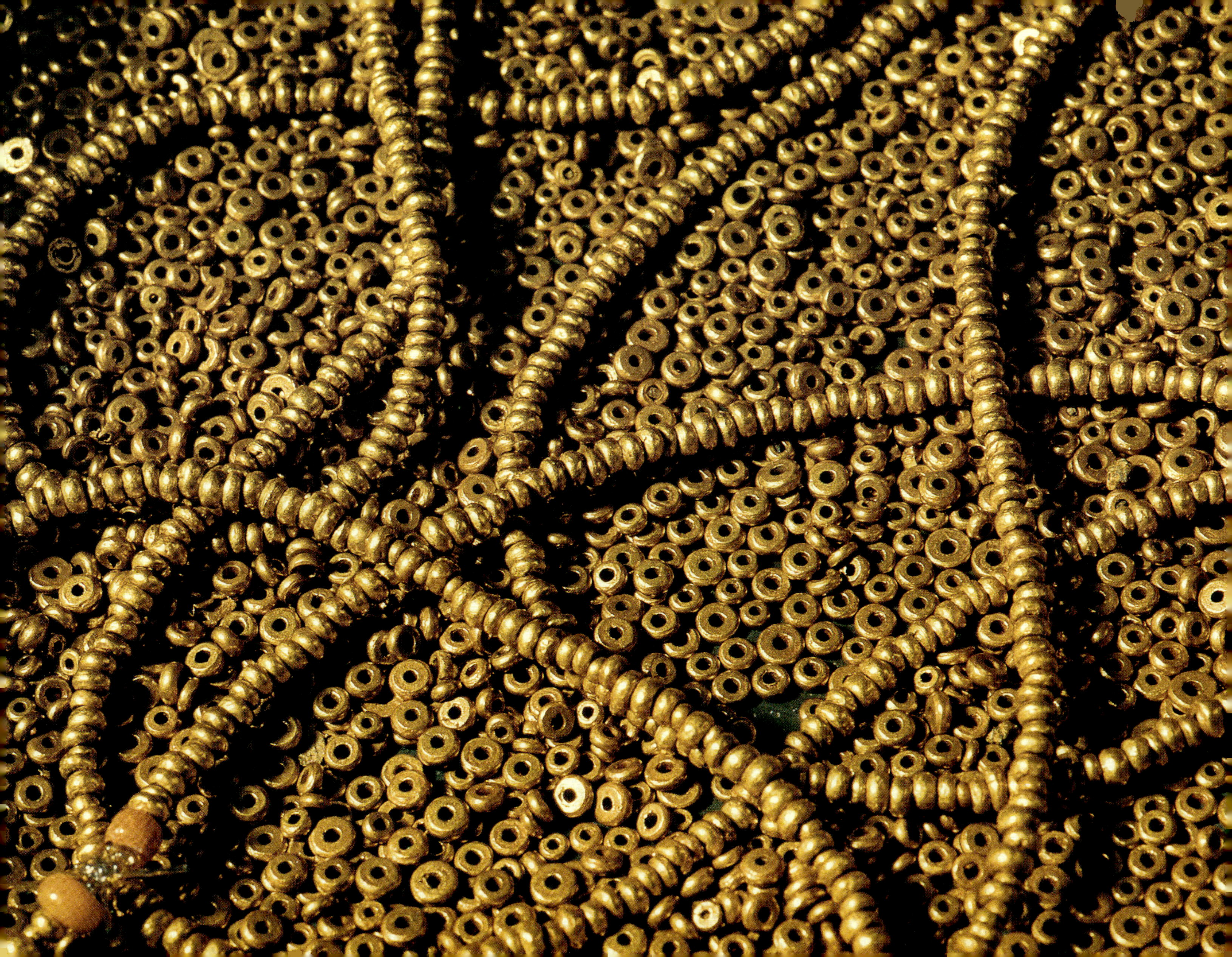

ABOVE Many gold beads were manufactured by using the punching technique, while others were wrapped by bending pieces of gold wire into loops (left). Some larger beads were individually cast, while were hammered flat and decorated with grooves. These methods, although seemingly simple, would be challenging even for the most skilled goldsmith today. The smallest gold bead at Mapungubwe measures less than one millimetre in diameter.
OPPOSITE Wrapped beads were made from gold strip or short lengths of gold wire, which were hammered rather than drawn. There is no evidence for wire drawing at Mapungubwe, and all the wire appeared to have been hammered and, in some cases, coiled.

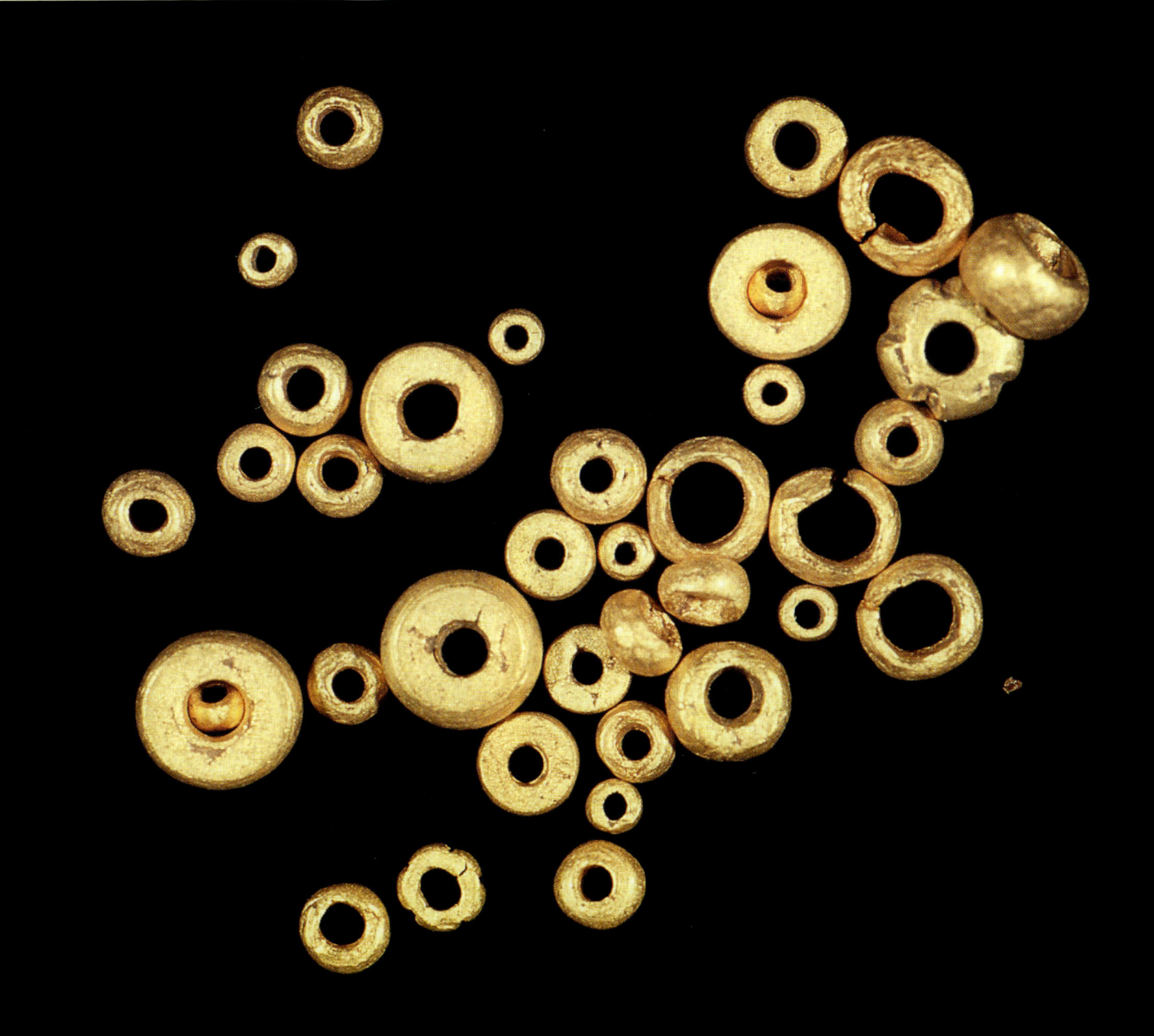

MAPUNGUBWE 39

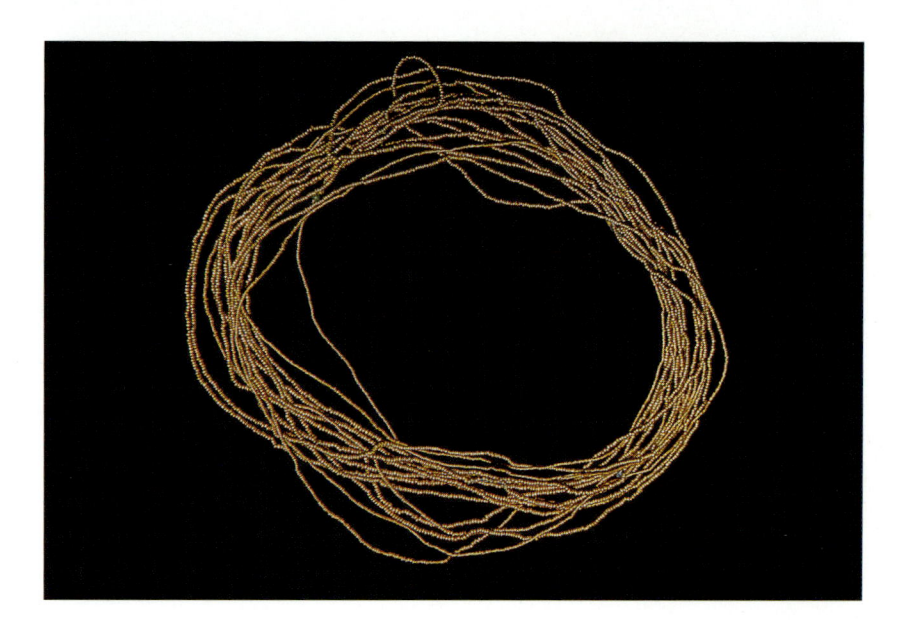

THIS PAGE *One of the gold burials on Mapungubwe Hill contained 2.2 kilograms of gold and over 12 000 gold beads. Literally thousands of these individual gold beads, once strung as necklaces or bangles, were recovered from a single grave. Gold beads were of great importance in a traditional society, and serving a purpose far deeper than mere ornamental jewellery or body decoration. Gold beads served as an outward sign of marital and social status, reserved usually for women of royalty.*

OPPOSITE *This multi-stringed gold-beaded necklace is made up of about 8 950 gold beads, individually and meticulously excavated and patiently restrung onto thread. It was probably worn by a female member of royalty, serving a social purpose of adornment or ritual rather than for its mere economic value.*

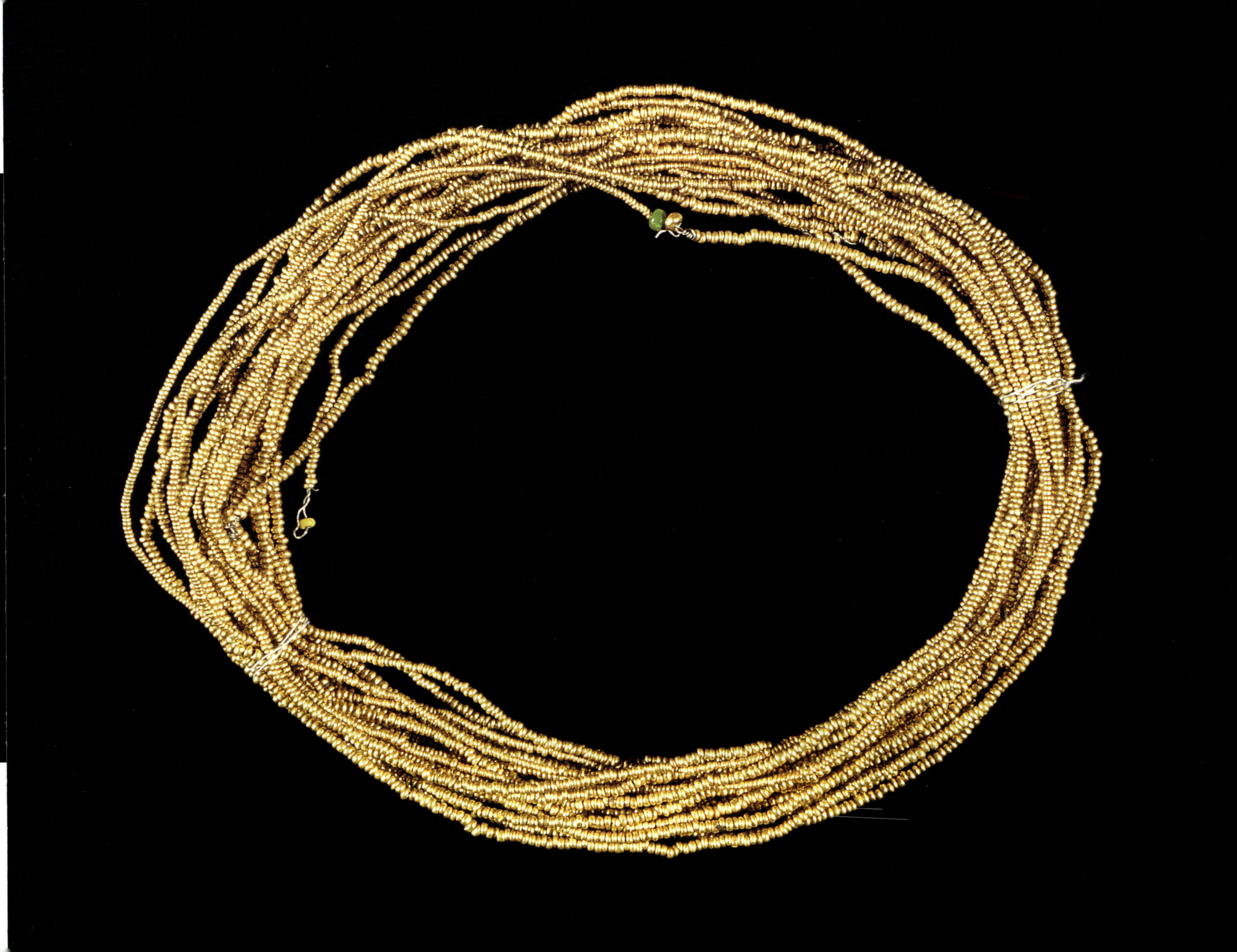

TOP LEFT The most remarkable of the indigenous glass beads were manufactured at K2. Craftsman melted down whole or broken blue trade glass beads and the molten glass was wound into clay moulds in which they set. When cold, the moulds were broken to free a large glass bead, known as garden roller beads. The translucent turquoise beads in the forefront are called vhulungu ha madi, or sea beads, as legend had it that the white man grew beads under the water and in Venda.
LEFT Various stones such as calcite and quartz, as well as marine shells, were also worked into beads and strung together with trade glass beads to create variety. It is doubtful whether these beads and the garden roller beads were, in fact, traded and seem to have only been used locally.
ABOVE The terrestrial land snail mollusc, known as Achatina immaculata, was used and manufactured into small shell beads predominantly found at K2. These beautiful shells clearly show signs of cultural modification and may have carried religious significance due to the frequency of their use as grave goods.
OPPOSITE The use of ostrich-eggshell beads is a time-forgotten tradition generally used among the Khoi-San. At Mapungubwe, however, some of the ostrich-eggshell beads seemed to have been deliberately burnt black to create a textured effect. These shells were found in vast quantities and were not only used as necklaces but also waistbands, which consisted of metres of beads wound into a band.

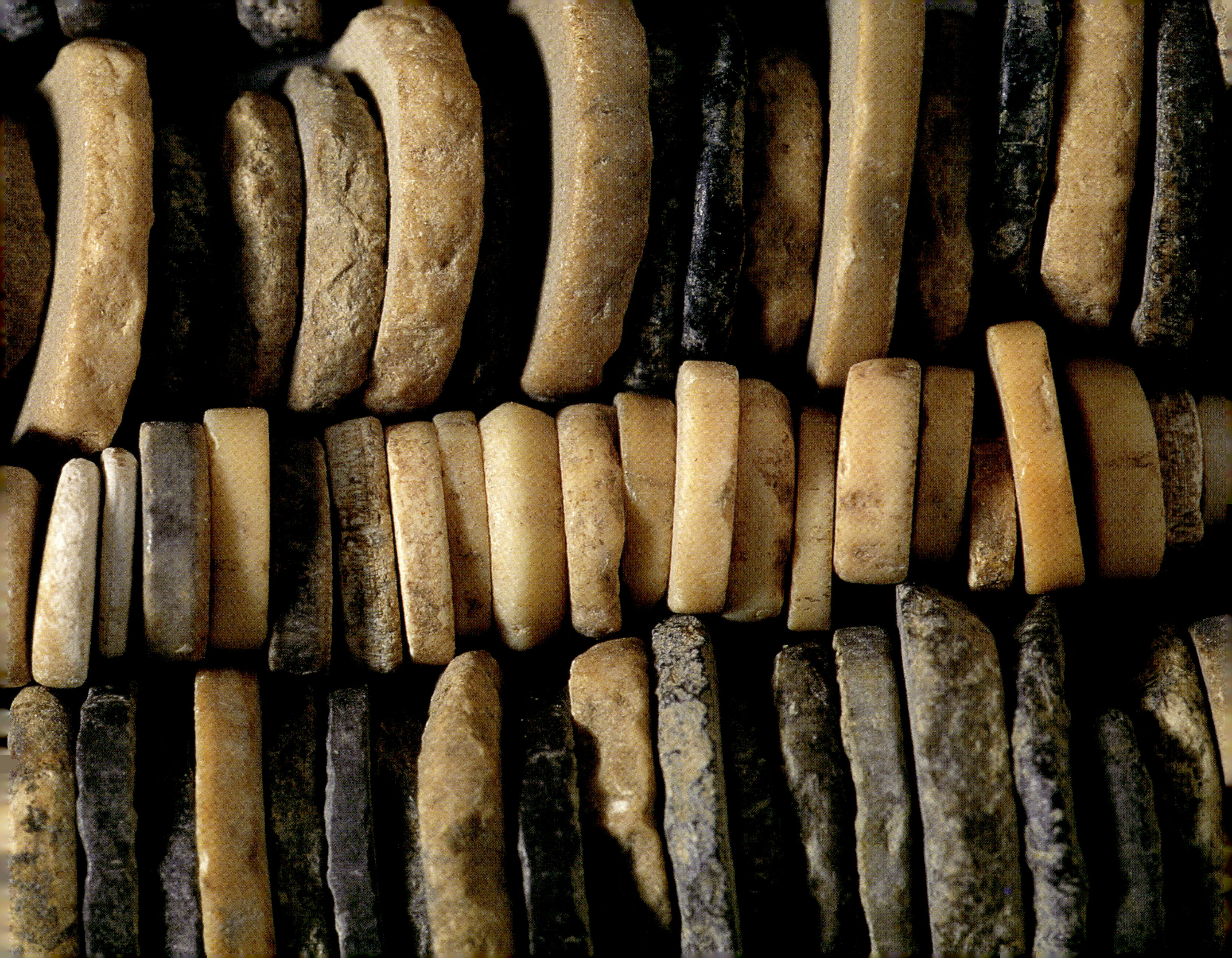

TOP This ingot is known among the BaVenda as a *musuku*. It is believed to represent the ancestors and was used as a commercial item of barter or trade. These ingots vary in size and shape. On top are studs, which usually indicated the amount of copper in the ingot. In many cases, one stud was equivalent in value to an iron hoe or a specific number of cattle.
ABOVE A few bronze items were also found, including this Swahili bangle.

ABOVE Besides gold, large quantities of other metals, such as finished iron and copper, were excavated at the Mapungubwe site. These were in the form of rings, links, wire, beads, plates, wound bangles, bracelets, arrowheads, small spearheads, hooks, nails, awls, pins, punches, chisels and blades. All metals would have been produced using a tool kit consisting of skin bellows, melting crucibles, stone hammers, anvils, iron chisels, blades and punches. It is also known that while the colour of metal work is ritually significant, copper always overshadowed the social role of gold. Iron and copper were smithed into tools for agriculture and woodwork, weapons for hunting, or decorative or ritual ornaments, which served to symbolise the status of a community member.
OPPOSITE Most of the tools used to produce the gold ornaments have not survived the archaeological record. Gold does not rust, tarnish or fade like iron and copper – although copper does have natural conservative qualities. This iron hoe is the most complete agricultural implement of its kind to be found at Mapungubwe.

MAPUNGUBWE 51

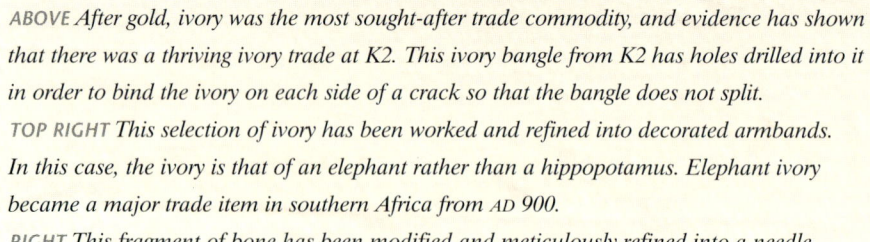

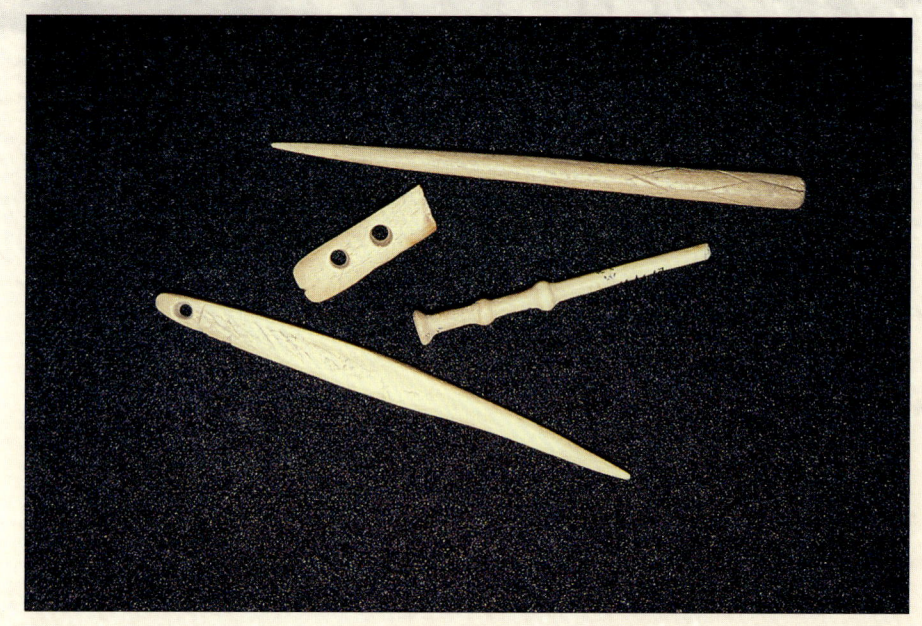

ABOVE After gold, ivory was the most sought-after trade commodity, and evidence has shown that there was a thriving ivory trade at K2. This ivory bangle from K2 has holes drilled into it in order to bind the ivory on each side of a crack so that the bangle does not split.
TOP RIGHT This selection of ivory has been worked and refined into decorated armbands. In this case, the ivory is that of an elephant rather than a hippopotamus. Elephant ivory became a major trade item in southern Africa from AD 900.
RIGHT This fragment of bone has been modified and meticulously refined into a needle with fine cross-hatch decoration and was most probably used in the preparation and sewing of animal skins.

ABOVE *Functional bone points, awls, needles, and hairpins were painstakingly fashioned from the bones of animals. Polished bone arrowheads and bone-link shafts, similar to the arrows traditionally used by the San people, were also deftly crafted and decorated for hunting purposes.*

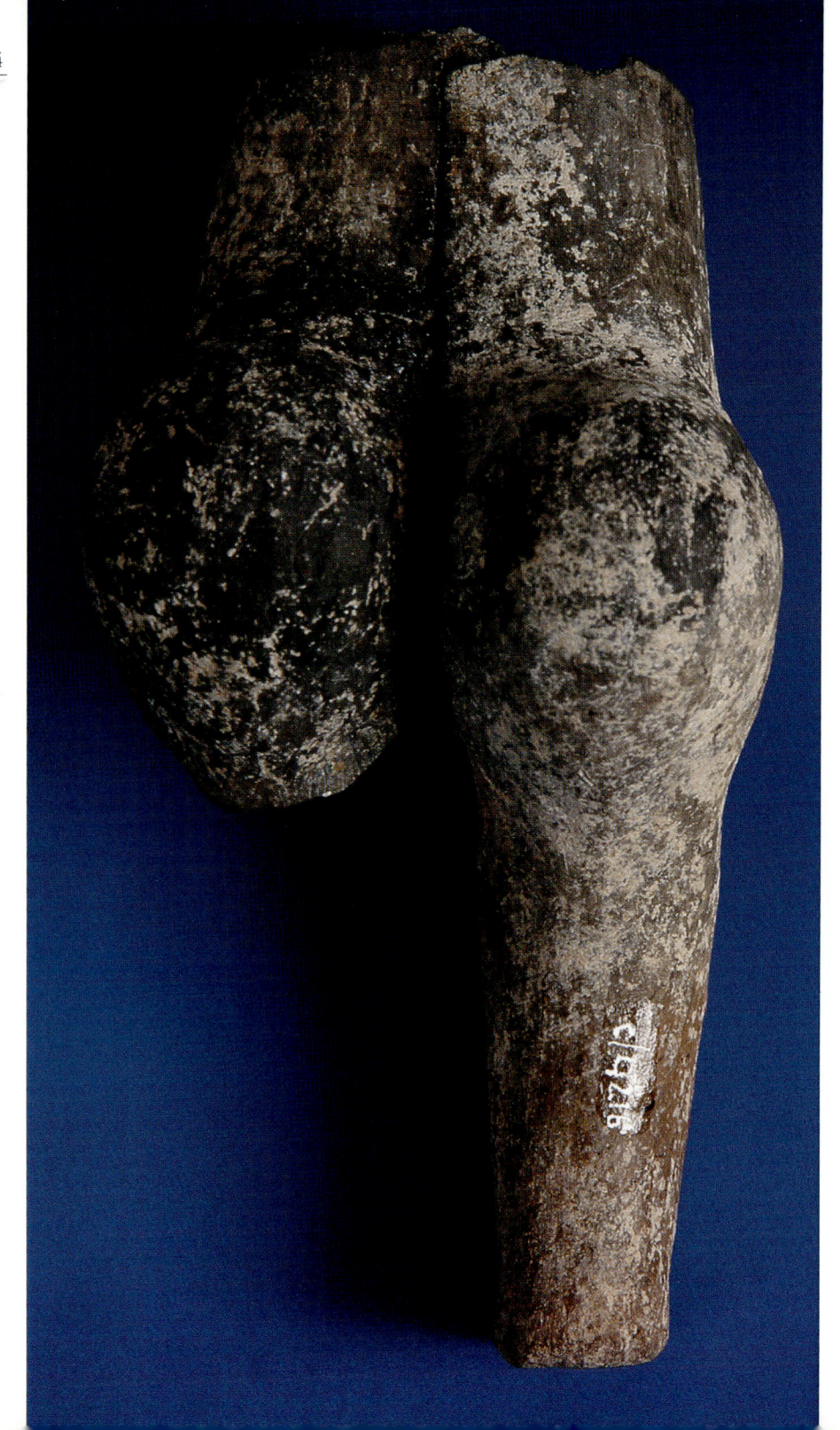

LEFT Clay figurines of the human form, mostly from K2, depict the female body. Clay was sculptured to shape small protuberances for breasts, a navel (umbilical hernia) and torsos impressed or incised with decoration. The distinctive patterns on the back, sides and around the navel are possibly reminiscent of the scarification marks on female inhabitants.
ABOVE These pendant-shaped ceramic objects are uniquely crafted and decorated whistles, perhaps used by a herdsman for summoning cattle. They were found on Mapungubwe Hill and are rather rare objects, not usually found in South Africa's Iron Age record.
OPPOSITE The fragments (far right) of Chinese Sung celadon ware (AD 960–1279) were found at Mapungubwe and are identical to the celadon wine kettle from the Van Tilburg Museum. This museum, also located at the University of Pretoria, showcases the largest ancient Chinese ceramic collection in Africa, donated to the university by JA van Tilburg. The celadons in this museum provide valuable comparative ceramics to the Mapungubwe celadon sherds.

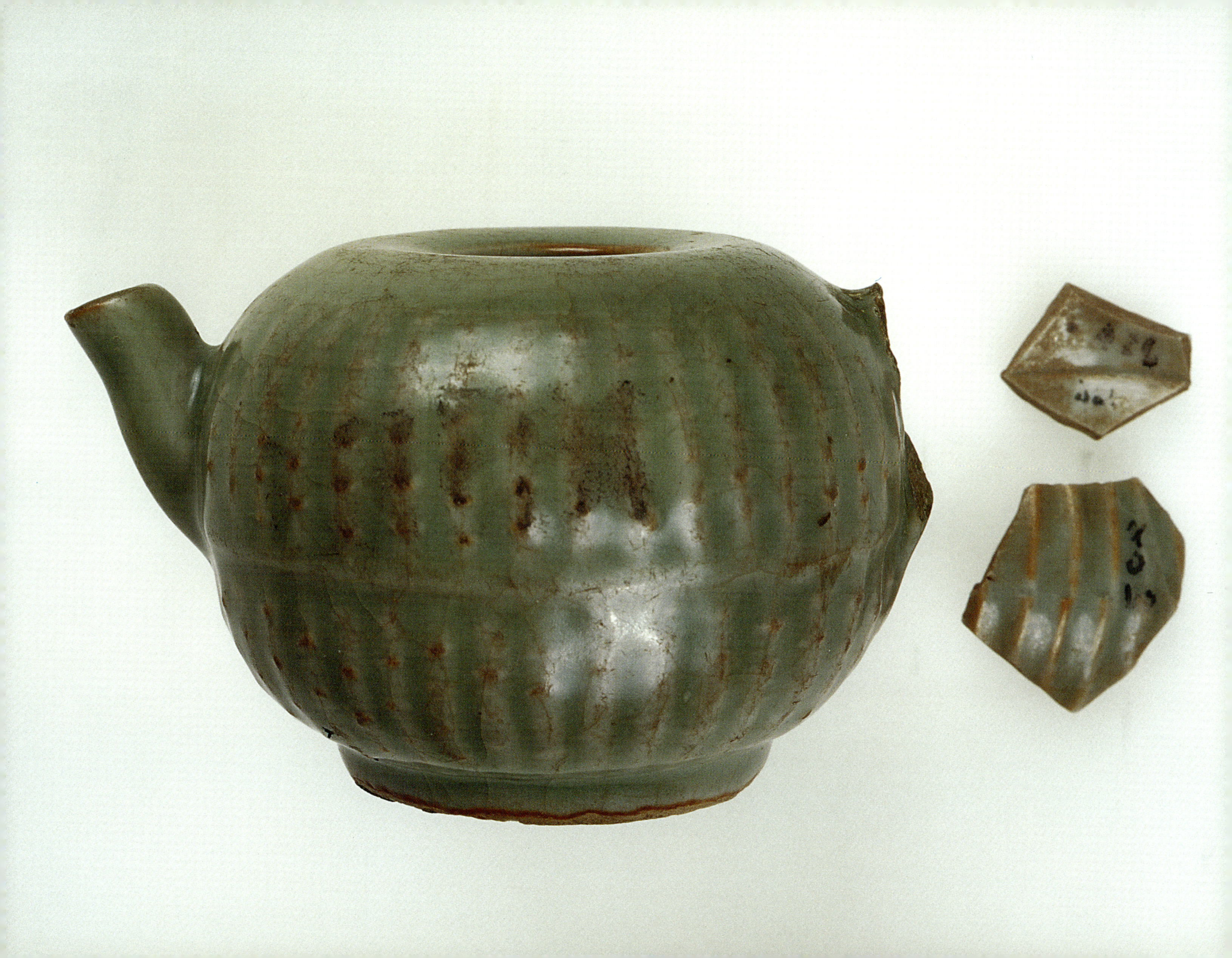

ABOVE Human clay figurines, generally from K2, come in a variety of shapes and sizes that vary from no more than 3 centimetres to 15 centimetres. Some figurines are depicted as half human and half animal. Other conical-shaped figurines, or phallic symbols, are thought to be associated with male and female initiation ceremonies, where they were used to demonstrate points of instruction, and illustrate life skills, family histories and traditions.

ABOVE *Nearly all the figurines originate from K2, and only a handful were found on Mapungubwe Hill. This human figurine, with a rounded head and stubby arms and legs depicting no specific gender, is unlike the other human forms found. Conical shaped figurines, ceramic spindle whorls used for spinning cotton, ceramic stoppers and a few animal figures were also found.*

LEFT *Most clay animal figurines depicted are domestic animals,. However, one of the most remarkable figurines is that of a wild animal: a giraffe. The small clay giraffe is very well proportioned, with an elegant, elongated neck and its curled tail held above the rump, a position it would hold while running.*

ABOVE *Perhaps one of the most rare clay figurines in the collection is K2's stylised hippopotamus or crocodile, which has a human torso and green trade glass beads pushed into the clay to represent its eyes.*

OPPOSITE *Clay animal figurines such as cattle, goats and sheep probably depict the domestic animals kept by the people at Mapungubwe and K2. Many of the cattle figurines clearly display a pronounced hump behind the head, indicative of the Sanga breed found in Africa. Figurines are modelled with such precision that the udders of cows, female goats and even the dewlaps of cattle are clearly portrayed. Sheep figurines have a distinctive shape and depict no tail, indicating that these Iron Age communities may even have practised tail docking.*

MAPUNGUBWE 59

A number of everyday, practical ceramic items, including miniature bowls, spoons, whistles, clay stoppers and clay earplugs were also discovered.

ABOVE This small, hand-moulded ceramic container is no bigger than 5 centimetres.

TOP RIGHT This cordage was from excavated from Bambandyana. Organic remains are a rare find.

BOTTOM RIGHT Small, flat, donut-shaped spindle whorls from Mapungubwe and K2 were fashioned from either ceramic or stone; some were decorated with incisions drawn into the wet clay. These were used to spin textiles – in all probability, wild cotton. This is a slow, painstaking process requiring specialised skills, probably a craft practised solely by women. The spindle whorls at Mapungubwe represent early evidence of a weaving industry. Even fragile fragments of woven basketry have survived.

OPPOSITE A miniature ceramic bowl (top), ceramic stopper (left) and a ceramic spoon (bottom right), possibly used for snuff.

61

ABOVE *The Mapungubwe and K2 ceramics, together with agricultural activities, were attributed to the labour of women. Part of pot-making is traditional knowledge of the soil and the selection of clay, which eventually determine the texture, shape and firing of the ceramic pot. Ceramics, decorated and undecorated, took the form of spherical pots, shouldered pots, shallow bowls, deep bowls, subspherical bowls, beakers, flat dishes, round and wide-bellied pots and spouted pots... the varieties seemingly endless.*

OPPOSITE *Spouted pots are rare in the Iron Age archaeological record and these spherical, neckless, undecorated pots with cylindrical spouts originate from K2. They were probably used for brewing traditional sorghum beer. A steaming process was used to extract alcohol coming from the spout. Communities usually call a pot by a name that indicates its shape and the use to which it is put; for example, in Zimbabwe, a ceramic pot in which beer is stored is called* mbiziro, *while the Sotho word for drinking is* bizo.

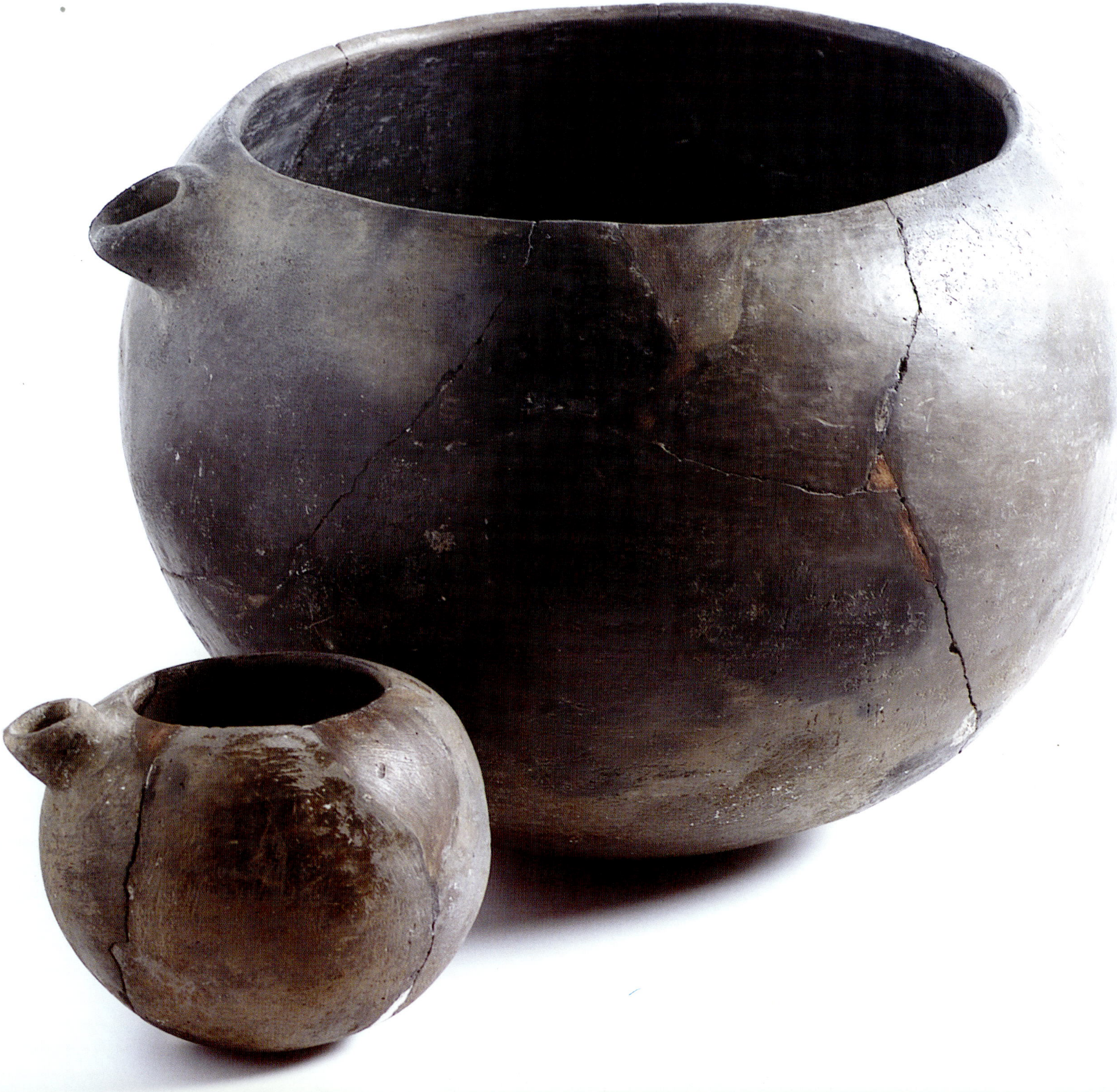

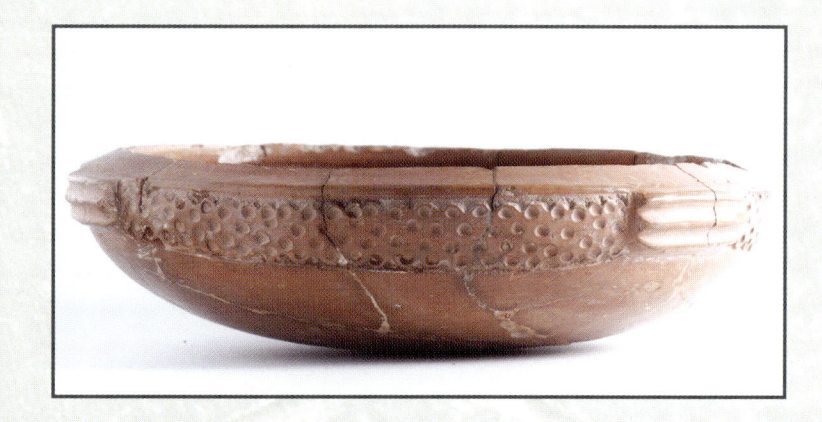

LEFT *Pottery was an important aspect of the everyday life of Mapungubweans and, likewise, remains a reliable clue to the archaeologist studying this ancient community. A single sherd can, for example, be a valuable tool in reconstructing the ways of life. This is a reconstructed ceramic beaker extracted from K2.*
ABOVE *Perhaps one of the finest ceramics from Mapungubwe Hill is this shallow terracotta bowl, which served as funerary ware. This unique bowl was elaborately described in 1937 as 'having a fine matt Indian Red surface with a bevelled rim to the outside, and is divided by three projecting lugs, each of which has two deep rounded grooves on the face and lightly scratched chevron along the surface of the bevel. The panels between the lugs are decorated with impressions of a round stylus made in the wet clay, and a festooned effect is produced by making them narrower at the ends than in the middle.'*
RIGHT AND OPPOSITE *These shallow bowls with slight black-burnt, umber surface finishes are decorated with chevron and diamond incisions and were found in the grave area on Mapungubwe Hill.*

MAPUNGUBWE 65

LEFT *Archaeological ceramics are classified according to the profile of the vessel: their shape, their rims, the nature and quality of the clay and decoration, textures, decorative techniques and added features, such as spouts, lugs, handles, bases and perforations.*

BELOW *The symmetry of the large hand-made ceramics from Mapungubwe is remarkable. The thickness of the clay, the finish of the surfaces and the precision of decoration is commendable. This large wide-bellied pot from Mapungubwe Hill has a series of diamond- and triangle-shaped incised decorations, and was probably used to store water. The girth and closed neck of the pot were designed to keep the liquid cool.*

OPPOSITE *This large subspherical bowl from Mapungubwe Hill is typical of the Mapungubwe ceramics, which differ from the vessel shapes and decorations unearthed from K2.*

MAPUNGUBWE 67

THIS PAGE *Literally thousands of pottery sherds were excavated and, in some fortunate instances, even complete ceramic vessels – unbroken over a 1000-year period – were uncovered. In most cases, ceramics were purely functional and served as cooking pots, drinking cups or storage containers for food, water or beer. This selection of small-shouldered pots from Mapungubwe Hill were probably drinking cups. The decorations on these seem more refined – for use by royalty – than other ceramics found at K2.*

ABOVE By tracing the decorations on sherds and the distribution of ceramics, one can tell a story of human progress and deterioration. With hundreds of decorative variations, the ceramics are characterised by incised, geometric patterns with cross-hatching and parallel grooving and diagonally incised triangles etched into the wet clay. These two beaker-shaped ceramic bowls are characteristic of the K2 ceramic tradition.

ABOVE AND TOP RIGHT *Complete ceramics or pottery sherds are the most common cultural material found at an archaeological site. Preserved in the middens or found in burials, practically indestructible and available in vast quantities, ceramic sherds belonging to varied vessels provide details about the Mapungubweans' traditional way of life.*

OPPOSITE *Six rather bizarre graves at Bambandyanalo, known as the 'Beast Burials', contained cattle bones that were deliberately buried with layers of potsherds, spouted pots, copper bangles, land-snail shells, cowries, glass beads, dismembered bones of rodents and pigs, and pieces of mica placed inside bracelets. When reconstructed, the ceramic sherds reconstituted 14 pots.*

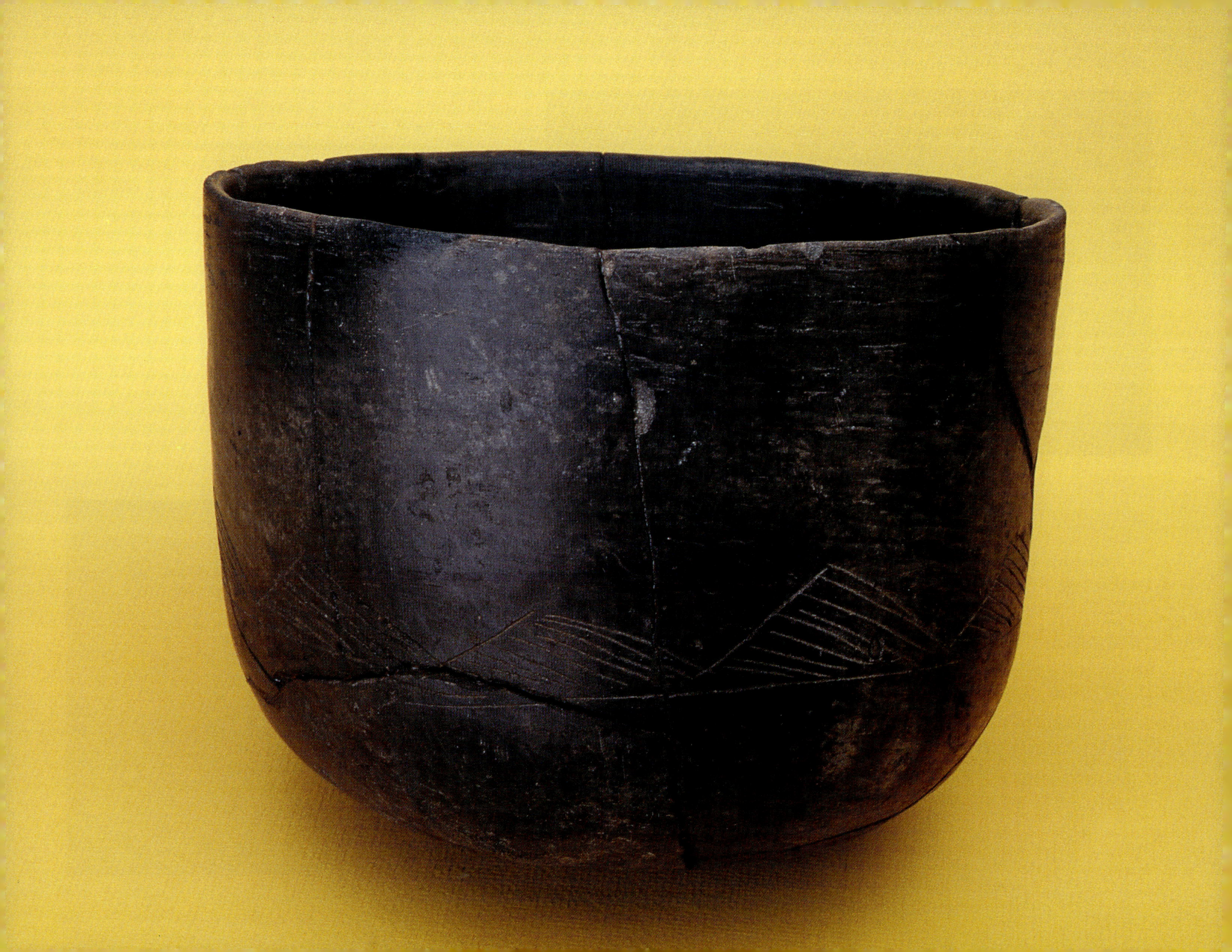

OPPOSITE *This white-washed (probably a mixture of clay and ash) shouldered pot was excavated complete, with burnt sorghum remains inside. The charred remains of storage huts, stone granaries, grinding stones, iron hoes and spindle whorls were also found, showing that pearl millet, sorghum, several species of bean and cotton were also cultivated by these ancient communities. Pictured in the glass dishes here are (from left to right) burnt marula pips, beans and charred sorghum.*

ABOVE AND TOP RIGHT *These large shallow bowls were probably used as containers for dry foods such as sorghum, millet and other edible grains. The women in this society were both potters and planters, as farming and pottery were closely associated. With the development of agriculture, vessels of this kind became a necessity.*

RIGHT *The ceramic pot on the left is white-washed with clay and ash, while the larger vessesl has been burnt black from cooking.*

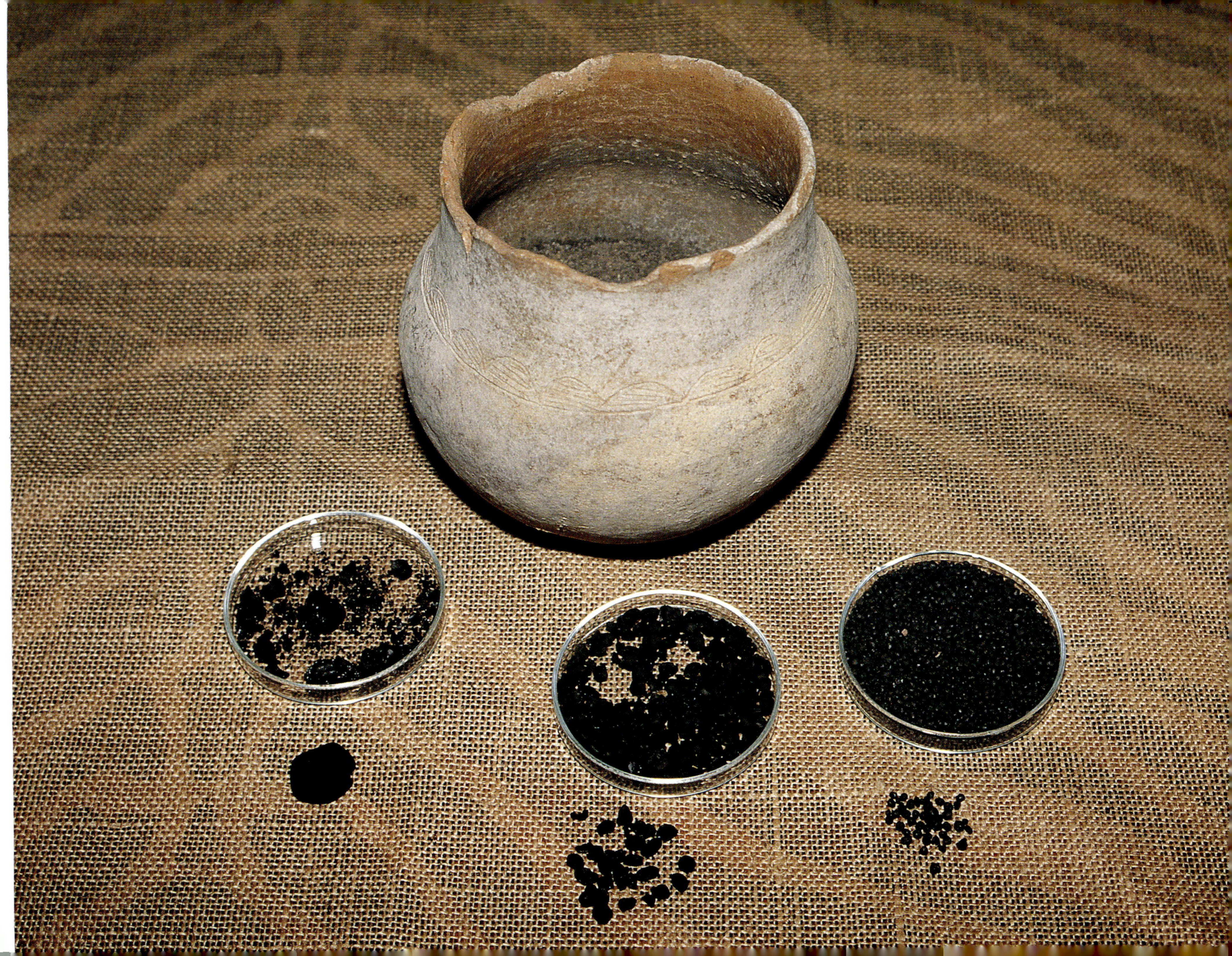

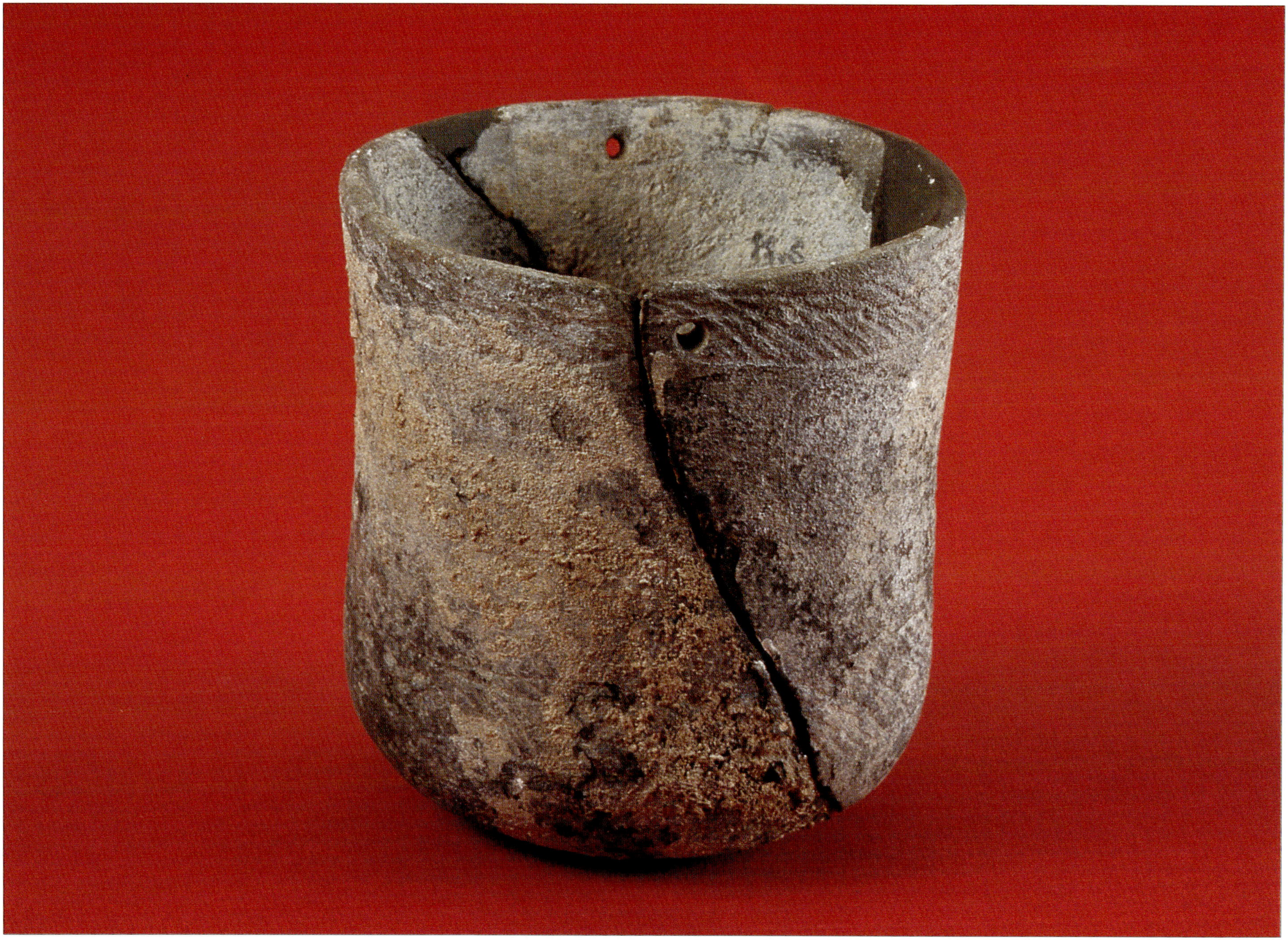

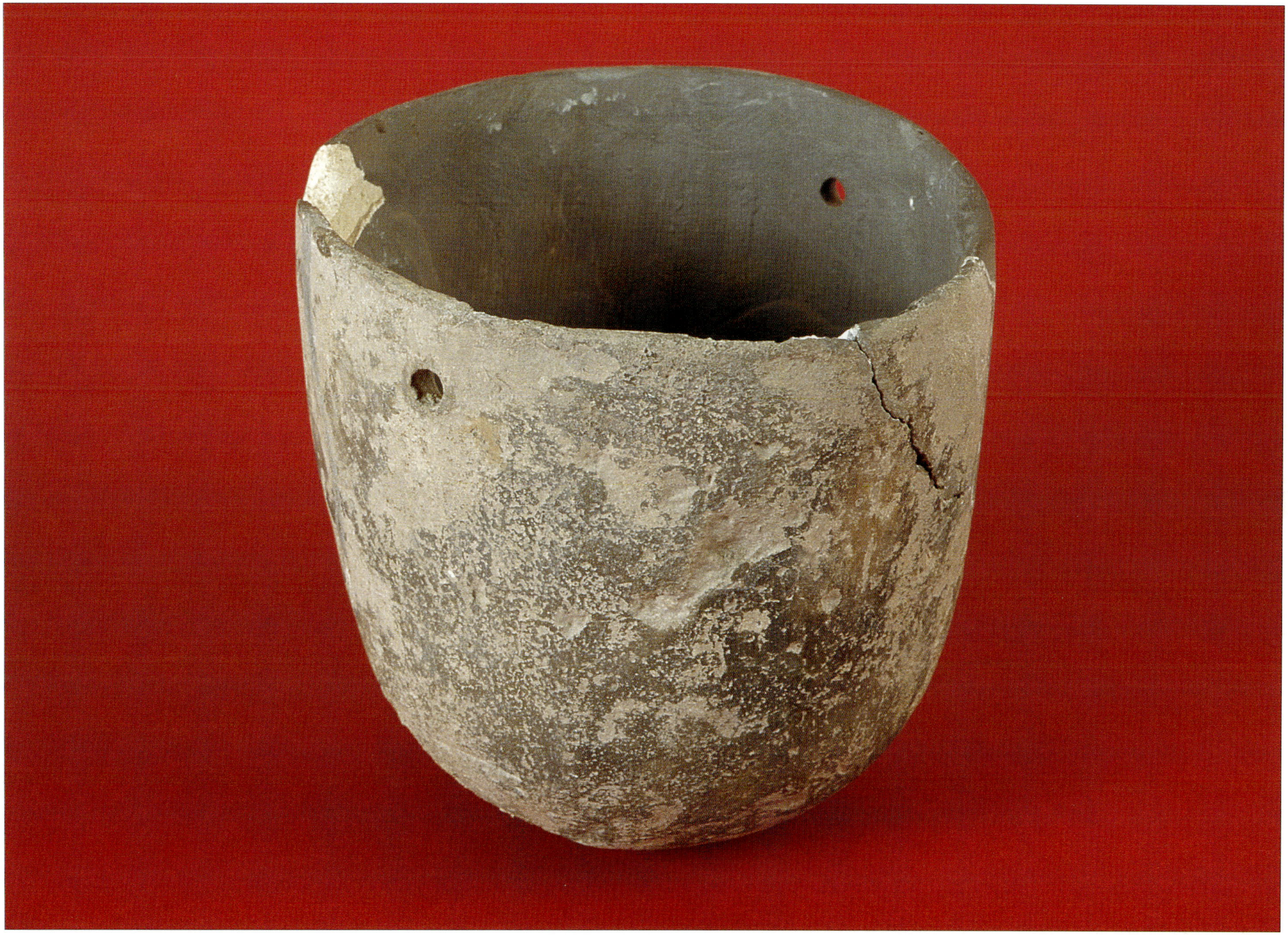

THESE PAGES Many beakers were manufactured with knuckle-shaped protrusions known as lugs or bosses on either side, and were used as drinking cups. Most decorations were engraved directly onto the burnt clay after burnishing. Beakers, in particular, are associated with the graves of people from the K2 period of occupation.

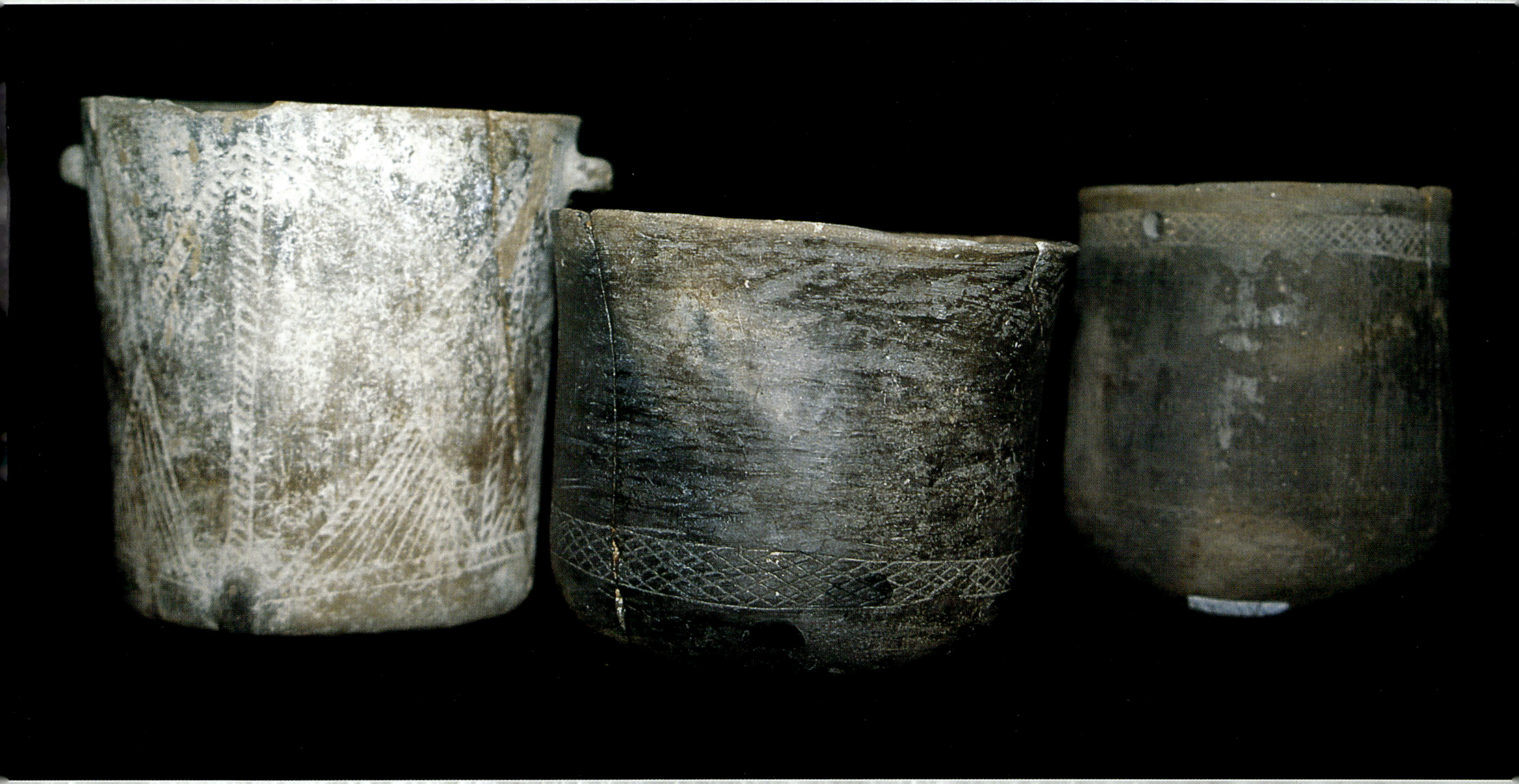

ABOVE Early excavators working on Mapungubwe Hill removed this stone board game in the 1930s. This ancient game is known locally as mankala *or* marabaraba. *Rows of shallow holes are pecked or engraved directly into the stone and rounded river pebbles are used as 'draughts'. It is interesting to note that versions of the game, played exclusively by men, are still played to this day throughout Africa.*